CW00952927

Diary

of

a

Stroke

Also by Jeremy Hooker:

from Shearsman Books

Upstate: A North American Journal
Openings: A European Journal
Ancestral Lines

from other publishers

Poetry
Landscape of the Daylight Moon
Soliloquies of a Chalk Giant
Solent Shore
Englishman's Road
A View from the Source
Master of the Leaping Figures
Their Silence a Language (with Lee Grandjean)
Our Lady of Europe
Adamah
Arnolds Wood
The Cut of the Light: Poems 1965-2005
Scattered Light

Prose
Welsh Journal

Criticism
Poetry of Place
The Presence of the Past: Essays on Modern British and American Poetry
Writers in a Landscape
Imagining Wales: A View of Modern Welsh Writing in English

As editor:
Frances Bellerby: Selected Stories
Alun Lewis: Selected Poems (with Gweno Lewis)
At Home on Earth:
      A New Selection of the Later Writings of Richard Jefferies
Alun Lewis: Inwards Where All the Battle Is: Writings from India
Mapping Golgotha: A Selection of Wilfred Owen's Letters and Poems.
Edward Thomas: The Ship of Swallows

For Mieke

Foreword

Within quite recent years, I was surprised to find some diaries that I'd kept when a boy. There was little that was surprising about the contents, with their references to school and fishing and playing with friends. What surprised me was the recognition of continuity – how much of my life has been spent recording it. As a student, inspired one day by a sense of wonder, I took up writing a diary again. The impulse soon failed among self-recriminations for boozing and wasting time. What I more grandly called a journal began seriously in the autumn of 1969, when I moved with my then wife into a small cottage in the hill country some miles outside Aberystwyth, where I was teaching at the university. Since then, with the exception of one period of a few months, I have kept a diary regularly, sometimes every day, and seldom less often than two or three times a week.

Since keeping a diary has become second nature to me, I've seldom asked myself why I do it. In 1969 the choice to start again was quite conscious. I wanted to observe closely the life of the new place in which I had come to live – the life of the natural world, and the culture of my mainly Welsh-speaking neighbours. I recall seeing an unfamiliar moth on the cottage wall, identifying and recording it. I borrowed a scythe from a neighbour and learnt to use it on the long grasses over-running the garden. It seemed important to record these things. I had been ill, and was now being restored to life.

Finding something to observe most days, I also found observation giving rise to reflection. This took my mind back to the earliest influence upon both my seeing and my writing: the essays of the Victorian poet-naturalist Richard Jefferies. I realized how for him perception of nature in all its living particulars had produced ideas; how in the relationship between the emotional, the seeing and feeling man, and the world around him, notation of the living moment had been the spark of thought. I never consciously read other writers' journals in order to open myself to their influence. I did however come to love the literary journal as a form practised by writers such as Dorothy Wordsworth and Coleridge, and Thoreau and Emerson. Moreover, I saw the close relationship between journal entries and certain kinds of poetry – different kinds, but with affinities based upon perception of the particular moment, as in Thomas Hardy and William Carlos Williams. In my own writing, a close relationship evolved between poem and diary, a relationship I would come to think of as an art of seeing.

When my stroke occurred without warning in July 1999 I was in the midst of a busy working life. I was teaching literature and creative writing full-time at Bath Spa University College. I was at work on a collection of poems and a critical book concerned with modern Welsh writers in English, such as Emyr Humphreys, Alun Lewis, John Cowper Powys and David Jones. Immediately before the stroke, I was preparing a lecture for a conference in London, and thinking about the speech I would make when we presented Fay Weldon for an honour at the university. I was aware of certain stresses in my personal life, but nothing prepared me for the experience that one morning I would wake up, walk with difficulty to the bathroom, fall over and just manage to crawl back to bed. Some hours later, in hospital, shocked but conscious, I asked a nurse if she would kindly bring me some writing materials. She brought me a sheet of paper and a pencil. For me, looking around as much as my weakness would allow me, and recording what I saw and heard and thought, was the natural thing to do.

The writing that resulted was ultimately a diary with a difference. As time passed and I became stronger, initially in hospital and then at home, I found that moments from the past were coming back to me; at first unexpectedly, they would rise in my mind: 'scenes', but quick with sense and laden with meaning. The moments belonged mostly to my early years, and involved people closest to me, my parents and grandparents, my brothers, my first friends. As they came back to me, so I wrote about them, and found myself composing a memoir, a fragment of childhood autobiography. The remarkable thing about this was that the focus of attention arising out of the diary form enabled me, at first unconsciously, to evade the self-censor.

I had never expected to be able to write about people close to me with any freedom. I have an aversion to confessionalism since it seems to me to slip easily into a form of betrayal, describing the other person – perhaps a parent or lover – from a single point of view, charged with personal emotion, and necessarily external. I have to say more than this. From the beginning, my instinct as a writer has been that of respect for the mystery of being in the unique person or thing. It is a disposition towards both world and words: a recognition of the reality words may point to, but cannot capture. As a poet I love language and value poetry highly as an exploratory art. At the same time I have an acute sense of the partiality of all forms of knowing.

In a poem of the Welsh hill country, I wrote once of a buzzard's cry 'confirming silence under all'. This describes my sense of the elusive nature of reality, of depths we may be aware of but cannot know. At a crucial time in my life, when suffering the consequences of introversion, I discovered the I and Thou thinking of the Jewish philosopher Martin Buber, with its emphasis upon relationship, and the importance of the 'between', where meaning is to be found. Buber is quintessentially a thinker who values community: the world we share, as distinct from the world disembodied in any one mind. Later, I felt a close affinity with George Oppen's emphasis upon the value of the substantive, and his poetry of essential respect for that which is. The other great influence upon my later thinking does not contradict this sense of the real. David Jones, in his Preface to *The Anathemata*, speaks of attempting 'to make a shape out of the very things of which one is oneself made'. This points to an essentially exploratory art, in which the maker is part of a much larger subject, which he or she seeks to know, as distinct from imposing the self upon the world.

All this may perhaps be put more simply. I couldn't imagine writing about people I love, as if they could be captured in a portrait, let alone subjected to the moral judgement that writing necessarily entails. I couldn't do it until I found myself doing it, as the past pressed for expression. The diary form with its everyday particular urgency disposed of my fear of betrayal. This fear had nothing to do with anxiety about revealing secrets. It had everything to do with avoiding the risk of partial vision, which diminishes lived experience, and replaces the whole person with a verbal portrait. As I say late in the diary, my parents were great powers in my life. It is the integral power of the unique being that I seek to recognise in my writing. Following my stroke, the act of recognition was made more urgent by my circumstances. As daybook notes and reflections became memoir, so I was revisiting what mattered most to me in the light of an encounter with death. From this I learnt a greater freedom, so that later, in poems about my family, especially in *Ancestral Lines*, I could show more of their lives and of the life that had made me.

Acknowledgements

Without my wife, Mieke's, help I would not have completed this book. My friend, Lindsay Clarke, supported me by his close reading of the typescript. I am grateful to Literature Wales for a Writer's Bursary that enabled me to shape the writing in its final form.

16 July 1999

Royal United Hospital Bath

I felt physically weak when I woke up yesterday. This morning, I should have gone to London to give a paper on R.S. Thomas & Alun Lewis at a conference. But I felt weaker, and fell over in the bathroom. Unable to get up, I crawled back to bed.

Mieke called Dr Ellis who arranged for an ambulance to bring me here. (Lying in the ambulance, I found I could see out through the rear window, and looked, at an unfamiliar angle, at the road I usually take to work.) Here, I have had numerous tests including an ECG & a brain scan; and the doctors think I have had 'a minor stroke'. I am too weak to stand and my left side, hand & foot are weaker than my right. They are also paying a lot of attention to my diabetes, with frequent blood sugar level tests. M. has been wonderful, staying with me most of the time.

I know I have brought this on myself with bouts of intensive work, far too little exercise, and relative neglect of my diabetes.

Hospital time. There are several other mainly older men in the ward, but I feel too tired to talk now. Mortal men, mortal men. We are hearts brains kidneys lungs. I have never felt so helpless, but I know this is real, part of life, though here we think of dying, hoping to get better. And perhaps others too think: I will regulate my life differently if/when I go home.

Our Lady of Bodily Functions, pray for us.

17 July

Fine morning. Weak. Difficulty swallowing. Young man in near bed moaned and cried out all night. Brain cancer.

Window view: clouds coming on softly. 'O shit. O Jesus!' Birds flying across occasionally – big gulls, ducks. Trees visible across car park. One big dark-green horse-chestnut. Mostly I half sleep or watch clouds. Never so weak. In others' hands – kind, methodical nurses. Lee & Kate rang last night.

Alun Lewis's 'patience' – which ran out on him? There are times when one should just endure. Why should he take upon himself the burden of failure of Western civilization? He couldn't be animal.

One thing after another in past months. Anxious over presentation of Fay Weldon at Graduation. Now someone else's responsibility. At times in the night I couldn't believe this has happened to me.

12.30 Ate a good meal.

Is the person who has difficulties with the self most thoroughly a self? Because of that concern? Keats & Lewis in their letters are utterly distinctive *experiencing* persons. Both claim to have no identity – Lewis's 'some animation the world has set flowing'. Lewis is more self-conscious, Keats has a stronger sense of the other? Is it all a self-drama with AL, even India? I have never thought myself No one.

Nurses firm with man with headache. Clearly they think he complains too much.

Lovely visits from M. & Colin Edwards, with a bunch of flowers from his garden at Freshford.

18 July

Morning. Was got up into chair but felt faint & weak and asked to be put back to bed. The nurse who had got me up obviously felt alarmed, and guilty. She put an oxygen mask on me and I lay on the bed.

Cloudless blue sky, light breeze. Older men on opposite side of the ward lying sleeping, mouths open, like effigies. Do I look like that?

None of us will live for ever. In extreme weakness I was afraid. The other thing that bothers me is lack of bowel movement, & embarrassment at the means. But the nurses are reassuringly matter of fact.

Reading *In the Place of Fallen Leaves* I realise how critical I am: its charm fails to charm me. I want something with more life in it, less fine & clever writing.

Afternoon, after visits from Emily & Jason, & M.: the disturbing experience of lying in a warm ward, half awake, with three or four conversations going on around, waking to a fragment here, a fragment there, the mind making some strange different sense of them.

Once I woke up in the night and for a while had no idea where I was.

Evening: good talk with Richard Kerridge & Philip Gross.

19 July

Monday – sat up in chair from 7 to 10.

Anxiety over lack of bowel movements, or sudden eruption. Misplaced shame.

Lovely flowers from David Annwn & Lesley.

Sandy Arnold & John Burke to visit.

Message from M. in morning but no visit; hope all is well.

'He'll never be the same man again.' (Mother, after Dad's mild stroke.)

Third night beginning. Young man whimpering and crying out.

What a difference it makes: as a patronising nurse, who complains wearily of night shift work, goes off duty, and another, who brightly calls me 'sweetheart', comes on. The young man in pain, loudly abuses a nurse: 'Get away from me, woman'. I ring for a nurse to pull up my blankets which I can't reach.

I may be able to feel a little more power in my left foot & left hand.

20 July

Morning. Sitting on bed. Outside: tough-looking prickly yellow cow thistle alongside grey chippings on parking area. By ragwort. Wayside survivors in waste places.

M. to visit in morning. Philip twice, once when I was asleep. Left a note but I didn't see him.

Evening: moved to Albert Ward. Visits from Jane Garbutt, Richard, Philip.

21 July

New window view. Convolvulus in hedge, orange & green flag over construction site of hospital development, hills above Bath. M. a.m. Joe & Emily p.m. Lovely visit. Reading *Le Grand Meaulnes*.

22 July

Nightmare complete scan in the morning. Lying inside the scanner being bombarded by noises like road drills, I told myself nothing could be as bad once I was out of it.

23 July

Sometimes with a start of surprise: I have had a stroke!
    Yes, from neglecting diabetes.

The hills are shadows, and they flow
    From form to form, and nothing stands;
They melt like mist, the solid lands,
    Like clouds they shape themselves and go.

24 July

When I lie within my bed,
Sick in heart and sick in head,
And with doubts discomforted,
Sweet Spirit comfort me!
    (Robert Herrick, 'His Litany to the Holy Spirit')

    Disappearance or dissolution of person (?) in the creative act (Nielsen).

Visits from Lee over the weekend, coinciding with a visit from Norman
Schwenk on Saturday. Blessings of friendship.
    Lee brought photos of his new work – the next step. How often we say
the same things in different words, or not quite the same language.

26 July

A run (pushed in a wheelchair) to the Vascular Unit for a scan. Glimpses of
the outside, different views, refreshing air.

27 July

Old man, blindly stubborn, out of bed, moaning, hitting nurse, poking
oxygen mask of neighbouring patient, confused, impossible. 'Where do
you want to go?'

Leaves shining in morning light.

Dressed myself in pyjamas.

To Sandy: 'I don't even know what diabetes is. Or insulin'.

Jim Insole in his wheelchair. Joe. Maddy. My granddaughter, bright Chlöe. All arrived in Maddy's van.

Tension in bed at night.

In extreme weakness one feels at the edge – facing into the dark. All metaphors for loss of consciousness. All words *in* life for something that is wordless – the feared nothing. Afraid, you know you are alive.

Written 28 July with a steadier hand.

Lying here I have received so much love.

Today is my 13th day in hospital.

It was 4.10 by the ward clock when M. first left me in bed – the blackest hour.

I read books, listen to music. Now, among other books, Peter Ackroyd's *Blake*. Ackroyd describes Blake as the last great religious poet. Nonsense. The last great biblical poet? Immersed in the Old Testament, moving in the world of its living figures. More alive to him than his fellow citizens – what men should be.

Late afternoon visit to Frome Hospital. The young ambulance man with whom I travelled knew Mieke, who started treating his daughter today.

Evening light through the ward window, at the angle at which I see it from home. I feel I could almost crawl there; but no I can't. My mind moves along the pavement.

From window at night, a bright planet.

Wheeled into washroom to wash myself. First time I have seen my face in two weeks – heavily bearded, familiar, quite healthy looking!

Visit from Lindsay Clarke who kissed me in greeting. He is working vigorously on his new novel and sounds fully involved in it.

Lindsay shared my dislike of Amy Michaels' much-praised *Fugitive Pieces*. His view seems to be that it is made of words, without felt life. I see it as a very clever literary concoction based upon research into several subjects which Michaels brings together and melds with reading Holocaust literature. How could so many critics be so impressed? Haven't they read the real thing, e.g. Primo Levi, which leaves no scope for aestheticizing the experience? To my mind Michaels' poetic style is self-cancelling: if every sentence is significant, none is. It is a novel full of human wisdom, often epigrammatically expressed, which, to me, doesn't ring true.

At the same time as I write I have been worrying that I am too critical. But there is a difference between having a bullshit detector as a reader and having a critical eye for human behaviour – in being deficient in charity & compassion.

Colin came in late bringing me a book of Cartier-Bresson photographs to look at.

Here, in a long ward of the Victoria Hospital, among old men, there are views of roofs of Frome, and, to the side, a shady walk under pine trees in the park.

30 July

Physiotherapy in the morning. Exercising leg muscles. Standing holding bars against the wall. This is what I need. Sue used to say I should be interested in her profession. One ignores or neglects so much until one has need of it.

Card & touching message from Al-Anon group. Would have cried if I could have done so without it hurting – as often in these days when I am shown so much caring.

Visit from Philip & Zélie who brought me a beautiful piece of granite from Dartmoor – reds greeny grey sparkles of mica. Fits my palm.

31 July

Primo Levi's 'The Canto of Ulysses' (*If This Is a Man*). Levi remembering fragments of Dante, in Auschwitz: a measure of human worth & dignity, together with memories of his native mountains. Great poetry not only survives; it *is* the survival of values.

With the attendance of nurses & regular mealtimes & other rituals hospital is like a long flight on an aeroplane, though not all of us are going to arrive anywhere.

Saturday morning visit from Emily & Jason.

On a hot afternoon my neighbour, John Burke, with his children Jack & Zoe, pushed me in a wheelchair round Victoria Park, immediately outside the hospital. Trees flowers lawns bandstand & war memorial. Distant views of Longleat & Cley Hill. Lords & Ladies. A robin in a birch-tree. John explained to me what diabetes is.

2 August

Long hot night. Loud voices of youths in the park until late. I could stand this morning with aid of bars in the toilet.

Reading a life of Richard Feynman: I simply don't understand why discoveries about the nature & behaviour of particles should, in the words of a scientist on the radio last night, 'kill deity'. It is the whole man, the whole human being that is involved in seeking a relationship with God. The excitement of scientific discovery may become a form of 'spirituality', but is inevitably a very partial one.

Partially sighted is what we all are. Scientific discoveries about the nature of matter explain nothing about ultimate meanings, and may only impress us by our own cleverness. To Blake, nature holds no secrets, only the Imagination perceives – creates? – spiritual truths.

A nurse tells me my left ankle is swollen, which sets me worrying. M. brings a bunch of feathery goldenrod & rich brown & gold sunflowers. Start Holmes's *Coleridge: Darker Reflections* & sympathise with STC's bowel pains on the voyage to Malta.

Quiet afternoon. Sky veiled, a little breeze stirring the sunshade on the walled seating area outside. Murmur of voices from a few visitors. Across the ward an old man lies with his mouth open, face sharpened, probably near death. Is it true that we imagine an afterlife mainly when we are in health, full of life, when it is hard to imagine anything else? How different, though, in extreme weakness, when that weakness, pulling one further down, is the only power we can feel!

I have enough strength now to know how weak I have been – the more strength to feel it, and to begin to feel more frustrated.

Late afternoon: physiotherapy – standing with hands on bed.

3 August

A cooler night. First rain for weeks. Vivid barely memorable sex dreams.

Physiotherapy with Ros Edwards. With Ros & Jane to help, walked with a frame to the end of the ward and back again!

Visit from Frank Kibblewhite in the morning. The last time he saw me I was full of vigour – talk & ideas anyway. Now, like Gerard, I am walking with a frame but, as Frank pointed out, Gerard won't be getting better. Frank is an exceptionally sensitive man, very sympathetic & intelligent.

> 'What no-one with us shares, scarce seems our own.'
> STC

Towering clouds. August cloud castles, moving slowly across the sky visible from the window, in the west.

Conversation with Jack, the old man in the bed beside me. Cancer. From Lock's Hill; he remembers Sunnyside and fields where council houses were built, on the Mount, from boyhood. Used to hear the clock of the old Asylum (across the road from where we live) at home in bed; delivered milk to Old Schoolhouse when he was a boy. A brave, down-to-earth man.

Afternoon: second walk of the day. Evening visits from my neighbours, Jenny & Paddy, and from Pip O'Callaghan, whose MA Project I was tutoring.

4 August

Fat pigeon cleaning itself with its beak, lighter grey plumage against grey pine bough stained with green lichen.

My earliest poetry was, very consciously, a form that excluded aspects of the modern world. In using the Chalk Giant & the shingle shore I aimed at a kind of integral language – not 'pure' in a puritan sense – which excluded the language & thought-world of advertising & popular culture, and enabled me to explore fundamentals uncontaminated. I didn't think exactly in these intellectual terms – it was more an instinct for a kind of unity – 'language' of materials & place – in effect also language of a loved 'world'. During that period I felt highly antagonistic to what I would now call (after Hegel) our age of prose, especially in respect of its buying & selling of human life & nature. I was influenced also by the models of

Lawrence & Hardy & their organic languages. Hence in part my attraction to the elemental as cosmic energies & grounded materiality. At times I have feared this has made me unhuman – the Robinson Jeffers view isn't mine – and retrospective; more in love with stones than people, and more concerned with a pre-industrial England than the present. I am not a snob but I have a horror of street-wise language & the argot of televisual culture. My view is that popular culture in all its forms betrays human beings and cheapens life.

Given this bias it was inevitable that I should think increasingly in Wordsworthian (*Lyrical Ballads*) terms. And at the same time become aware of self-imposed limitations – the limitations of the language I can actually use. Whatever the answer, becoming a 'new poet' making free with contemporary slang isn't it.

In part I found what I wanted in George Oppen, with the difference that he was American. On reflection, though, I can see that he though urban is elemental – perhaps all Americans are, because aware of American ground – soil, rock, sea – the great body of the continent itself, present everywhere, under the skyscrapers as in the country. What prevents English poets from feeling this in England is a state of consciousness, a habitual blindness. They are more social, but in a way that cheapens the social by dematerialising it – and despiritualising it – by abstracting it from the ground. This cheapening betrays democracy, in the Keatsian sense of a conversation of individual thinking & feeling beings.

More physiotherapy: walking with Ros. I feel my weakness, but am stronger. Even at the best of times I walk peculiarly, as Les used to like pointing out. Now my legs are being re-educated. Weak, a man can feel like a tree, heavy & in danger of falling under its own weight. John Barleycorn cut off at knee.

So far I can't share the biographer's tremendous enthusiasm for Richard Feynman. An attractive man, but why should a genius for physics be other than an extreme specialism which limits insight in other directions? Having fun as a relief from the Manhattan Project doesn't impress – but what would?

Opinion in the ward was divided over the Queen Mother's 99th birthday. Early in the morning a big bolshie nurse says indignantly that she too would be 'wonderful' if everything had always been done for herself. Later an older nurse remarks cheerfully to me on the event, as if I should find something to rejoice in in it.

Visit from Kim Taplin in the afternoon. She looks very well – always a good walker, but Jeremy is fanatical. She says she feels she hasn't woken up yet. How does one? I thought about my writing, always aiming to see more. But Al-Anon, and the last 3 weeks, have made me feel awake as a human being sharing life with others.

Therapists questioning an old lady with thin, badly ulcerated legs who has been brought into the ward:

> 'Are you worried about anything?'
> 'The state of the world.'

5 August

Heavy rain overnight breaking the drought. Mother's birthday: 5 August 1906, the weak baby they thought wouldn't live, and christened Ivy because (she said) it didn't seem worth giving her a more substantial name.

> 'Have mercy on me, O something *out* of me! For there is no power (and if that can be, less strength) in aught within me!'

> 'man's dependence on something out of him.'
>   Coleridge

In contrast, Blake's feeling (for it is first feeling) seems to be of self-sufficiency, the idea of gods being products of the human breast perhaps relating to the artist's constant self-reliance & productivity. It may be that the opposed views of Nature also derive from this difference – Coleridge (and Wordsworth) responding to 'something' in Nature, while to Blake Nature without the human imagination is nothing. My feeling is, and always has been, much closer to Coleridge's.

Richard Holmes connects Coleridge's belief in 'the one Life' with the idea that 'the earth [Gaia] might in certain ways be alive – not as the ancients saw her, a sentient goddess with purpose and foresight – more like a tree. A tree that exists, never moving except to sway in the wind, yet endlessly conversing with the sunlight and the soil'.

Another hospital day. Toilet, wash & dress myself. Visit from M. & Bethan & Ard in the morning. Reading. Listening to the rain – interrupted Test Match on the radio or watching it on TV. Regular meals. Monitoring my blood glucose. Sleep after mid-day meal. Two walks with frame. Visit from Sandy in the afternoon. She complimented me on my patience. But what alternative is there? (In any case, I would probably be reading if I were at home.) M. comes again in the evening. A fresher, cooler day.

At least I'm not here worrying that none of my poems is in any of the end-of-century anthologies.

6 August

An old woman was brought into the ward late at night. She soon began to cry out: 'Help me, please help me', then 'Please kill me off', 'Let me die' and called on her sons, daughter, her husband, her mother & father (who must be dead). All night, with intervals when she was probably asleep, she begged for help or to die. Nothing to do but listen.

Walk with frame to toilet & washroom in the morning – another first.

During the day the old woman lies, her face badly bruised, wearing an oxygen mask, across the ward. She is visited by three big sons & her daughter, whose names I heard her call over & over.

Morning visit from Elin, who arrived at Bristol Airport from Amsterdam at 9, with M. & Bethan & Ard, who return to the Netherlands today. I feel how lucky I am.

> 'Not justice nor enduring correctness endears to us the criticism of Eliot, Matthew Arnold, or Dr Johnson, but precisely the sense that, for them, criticism was being used in the service of a tremendous will to power, one desirous of rewriting literary history in order to leave a blank that the poet can fill.'
> Adam Kirsch, reviewing Randall Jarrell, *TLS*

Is this true? Can't a critic be passionately dispassionate?

Physiotherapy downstairs in the exercise room. After walking sideways supported by a kind of bed, a few unaided steps – Ros ready to catch me if I stumble – across a small space of tiled floor that looks like an expanse of desert. I am still often surprised, and sometimes, for an instant, think I could jump up and walk.

7 August

Heavy rain. Dawn with an old moon.

The old woman whined & moaned & talked all night. Impossible to shut out, but now, like the nurses, I felt exasperation not sympathy. There seemed something wilful about it, while my sick neighbours suffered in silence.

Holmes speculates that Coleridge's 'concept of the poetic imagination which acted as a single unifying force within all creative acts' owed a significant debt to Humphry Davy's 'scientific theories about the nature of energy and matter'. 'Davy supposes that there is only one power in the world of the senses; which in particles acts as chemical attractions, in specific masses as electricity, & on matter in general, as planetary Gravitation … When this has been proved, it will then only remain to resolve this into some Law of vital Intellect – and all human knowledge will be Science and Metaphysics the only Science.' (Coleridge)

Measure the distance between this and present-day theoretical physics with its passion for the invisible constituents of matter and contempt for mysticism. Coleridge, by contrast, hated 'the needlepoint pinshead System of the Atomists'.

From the window beside my bed – from which at dawn I saw the old moon – I can see, over part of a red-tiled roof & over tree-tops – fragments of the downs beyond Westbury, &, over them, slow-moving stacks of August cloud. This morning I made some kind of start – a few scratchy prosaic lines – on the poem for my father; but it's unlikely that I shall be able to write in these conditions. How lucky, though, that my mind has been unaffected – even when I could scarcely move a pencil or pen, I could still think, and speak.

Summer clouds in chalk country – for as long as I have loved these things, it has never occurred to me that, one day, I would be looking at them out of a hospital window, unable, if I wished, to walk over the hills.

8 August

Jack died yesterday evening. I felt he was a kind, strong man. The nurse who told me, after I had asked about him, said he had had a very full life, and knew that he was dying. (I had heard him ask: 'Am I dying?')

Opposite to me now is a young woman in her forties. I thought her younger – she has almost a girl's face. She told me she is a 'recovering alcoholic', and, six months ago, weighed 19 stone. She fell in the bathroom this morning and bruised her face badly. She means to live until the Millennium, she told me, and celebrate with a tiny amount of champagne in the bottom of a glass of orange juice.

The old woman died this morning. While Elin was with me, all the curtains round the beds were drawn, and her body was removed.

Before Elin came in, I was able to read the proofs of my essay on Geoffrey Grigson. What I can't do unaided yet is walk.

Afternoon visit from Anthony Nanson, a young novelist on the MA in Creative Writing. After I had given him an account of my progress we talked books & writing for an hour or so. Later, when Mieke came, rain was pelting down outside. I repeated to her what I had found myself saying to Anthony, that in some ways the last three weeks have been the best in my life: because I am so happy about Joe (and Mieke) and the effort to overcome addiction, and deeply touched by all the care I have received. Also, in a curious way, the time has been restful, with no pressure on me, and plenty of time to read, and talk to friends.

> 'To care about words, to have a stake in what is written, to believe in the power of books – this overwhelms the rest, and beside it one's life becomes very small.'
> Paul Auster, *The New York Trilogy*

9 August

Everything is damp this morning after torrential rain last night. (How beautiful the word *rain*, especially after a period of drought.) From the bathroom window, under grey skies, a clump of beech-trees crowning the far downs.

After talking with Anthony yesterday, and after reading different kinds of good fiction, I wonder again about my failure to write a novel.

The simple truth is: I lack the will. Writing fiction for its own sake, as it were, doesn't interest me, although I can appreciate the attraction for others, and enjoy the results. Perhaps also I have too large a sense of self, so that I think of my life in terms of a story, or several stories, rather than as providing materials that I should shape into fiction.

I would like to write something that contains a sense of life as I have experienced it, and of the lives of those I have come close to (from whom, indeed, my sense of life has derived so much); but this I already do, up to a point, in my journal. So it seems the kind of book I could write wouldn't be a novel in any usual sense.

Yet, if I return to this subject now, it's because I feel some guilt at not having made more of my ability as a writer. Coming close to death as it seems (but we are always close to death), I have thought of my work as though it were finished. It doesn't seem to me a poor thing, but as *less*; in effect, incomplete.

Incompletion, though, is the measure of most lives, as virtually built in to the human lifespan. Yet I'm not content with this formulation.

Do we ever think of the work of a true poet being incomplete? Even when we speculate, fruitlessly, about what Keats, or Wilfred Owen, might have written, we know their work has a completeness, or perhaps we mean an integrity: the whole nature of the man has been realized even in fragments.

The real question for me isn't comparative; it's about what I feel – which is that I still have a lot of work in me, and if I weren't to realize it, I would have let myself down; made a poor use of my time.

Even in thinking of myself as a potential novelist, I may be undervaluing poetry. A strange thought for one who is obsessed by it. It would be more to the point for me to think of imaginative exploration, adventure, form-breaking & form-making. Again, *The Marriage of Heaven and Hell* as inspiration – that excitement of broken limits, unexpectedness, invention; laughter of genius at little ideas of form. What I think of as possibilities of opening, as I have recognised it in David Jones, in W.C. Williams & other Americans: shapings that transcend the reach of any ego, that spring from, and go deeper into, life.

Old faces over the coverlets of hospital beds, bodies under sheets; faces concentrated in suffering, or drawn, sculpted, in sleep or semiconsciousness. How we see what we are: singular beings, isolated within ourselves, coming down to a final concentration – all we are in this body, this mind. Others gather round, reminding us we are not only this, but a man or a woman with family & friends, connected to the world. But still we are *this*, moving or drifting inward, away from all the world of light. Yet I do not accept it: this is not all. In truth, I know nothing except life, and life is certainly not this, concentrated in the sharpened face, the body more angular. I don't know what death is; but I-alone is death.

Silver lines of rain against dark green leaf masses. Leaves motionless except when one is struck. Silver drops falling from the edge of an outdoor table. It is colder now with the rain, almost autumnal.

> 'Strangers born in the *Mountains* are consumed in the *Lowlands* by an incurable homesickness. We are made for a Higher Place, and that is why we are gnawed by an Eternal Longing, and all the music we hear is the Cowbell that reminds us of our Alpine Home.'
>
> Jean-Paul Richter

> '…all the organs of Sense are framed for a corresponding World of Sense: and we have it. All the organs of Spirit are framed for a corresponding World of Spirit: & we cannot but believe it…And what is Faith? – it is to the Spirit of Man the same instinct, which impels the chrysalis of the horned fly to build its involucrum as long again as itself to make room for the Antennae, which are to come, tho' they never yet have been!'
>
> S.T. Coleridge (Both quotations in
> Richard Holmes, *Coleridge: Darker Reflections*)

Excursion to the Physiotherapy Department, across the yard, in an interval between the rain. Walking with the help of parallel bars, trying to set my feet down. A balancing act.

It's a curious thing but I can distinctly remember learning to stand. Crawling to Dumpty (first objects are beings) in the living room at Fairacre and hauling myself up by it. But this is different: standing now requires re-learning what I have been doing naturally since that time. Suddenly it's mechanical, conscious and feels awkward. All the same, a bit less so every day.

Afterwards Jim Dales, the painter, visited me. We first met a few weeks ago, at the launch of Crysse Morrison's novel, and he attended my talk on 'The Poetry of Landscape' at the Tippett Centre – when I felt full of vigour.

While I am interested in experimental poetry, I suspect that my own poetic impulses are really very simple. The roots are emotional & sensuous, and in a feeling for the life of nature & the land. I am drawn to the elemental & essential, to living rhythm & sculpted image. But if this is where it begins, it isn't where it ends. 'Natural' ways, in fact, are culturally conditioned – conventions of seeing & feeling, as in Georgian pastoral. Thus, to an extent, I struggle against what comes 'naturally', seeking an opening beyond myself, & a larger understanding of reality & the crisis of meaning I have inherited. The problem is how to draw on original impulses – child in man – while at the same time responding as a complete human being, with a fully engaged mind, to the world in which I live. I say 'mind' because I want to honour both intellect & imagination. In my view a lot of contemporary English poetry shows a failure of intelligence, as poets unconsciously exploit various conventional ideas of poetry, including the naively egoistic, & prosaic empiricism. I value lyricism, but resist the song that sings itself.

Sitting in this chair, I feel I know something of what my father in his last years felt. Except he seemed to be granted a large measure of oblivion – as we comforted ourselves & appeased our consciences by thinking.

His dead face with the artificial 'smile' was one of the strangest things I have ever seen. Not the man himself but a lifeless waxwork imitation. Living, he was a completely original person – even his borrowings were his own, like 'God's gift of seeing', which I later learnt (he never denied it) was John Constable's.

Is it sentimental to imagine we talk to the dead? The same could be asked of prayer, which to a non-believer would never reach beyond the privacy of the mind. Closed in that 'space' which in each is a locked room. It is hard for us to conceive of ends, because in nature there is no such thing. That isn't the only reason though, and in any case nature consists of material transformations. It is the reality of human personality that I cannot imagine being annihilated. Or perhaps I can imagine, but not accept it. How hard the spiritual is to believe in in our culture. We don't have to accept its limitations, but it gets into everything – language & thought are saturated with it.

10 August

Blood-sugar level higher last night. Medication increased.

An overcast day. Sycamore leaves, which I can see through the window, trembling & shaking.

I was tired after physiotherapy yesterday. Today, when I walked, my legs & feet were more flexible, I was less flat-footed, with a more elastic tread.

Afternoon. My first visit home, with the occupational therapist to assess the facilities that will enable permanent return, perhaps this weekend. And how homely it was, the front room like a comfortably lit painted cave, with our sculptures, paintings, furniture. As it always is, but I fail to see, taking it for granted. But now, although all was familiar, I saw it with a stranger's eyes, too.

The quality of NHS care, as I have experienced and observed it, is impressive. What a contrast with the past! I am reminded of Gillian Clarke's question in 'Letter from a Far Country': 'Before the Welfare State who cared/for sparrows in a hard spring?' At the same time I was reading about Lev Shestov and his contempt for the 'common' world. I understand this as a rejection of the assumptions & ideals that prevent people from really experiencing life. It is anti-rational & anti-bourgeois & anti-scientific. But insofar as it is anti-humane, I reject it. The truth is that organized care, the structuring of social institutions to provide care for those who need it, and to allow professional service to others, is lacking in poetic or philosophical glamour. This may be an unfair & even cynical way of putting it, but, from this existential viewpoint, the common bonds of humanity are overlooked, when they are not derided.

There is an alternative tradition, of course, in Wordsworth & the novelists & poets who follow him, in Whitman & Williams – ultimately, a Christian tradition, though often rejected by the socialists who owe a debt to it.

I am moved by the individual struggle. But I am more conscious of what we owe to the common, & the need to celebrate, & when necessary defend, what is so signally lacking in *romantic* attraction.

It is easy to admire heroic thinkers, Nietzsche or Shestov, but I believe in a climate of feeling in which we can also celebrate the engineers who constructed water & drainage systems, the founders of hospitals, the men & women who made possible the Welfare State.

The book about Shestov reminds me of Plato's assertion that true philosophers 'study nothing but dying and death'. My understanding of this is that death is the question behind everything. In that sense, although I am no philosopher, I assent to its truth. Less impersonally, I recognise that poetry, which is my thinking, takes place against the background of the fact of death.

There's nothing morbid about this. Life shines against the dark – that's a way of putting it. The sense of an ending quickens the need to be awake in the present, and to make something of it. Death makes me acutely aware of love & its poignancy.

This is no abstract statement. Every day recently I have seen the dying & the visitors who cherish them, and heard words that express all our inadequacy, the inevitable failure to reach across. These are our ordinary scenes, in which we are baffled, unable to prevent the once-in-a-lifetime event. And of course I have thought about – and feared – my own death, hoping it will be postponed.

Death is the mystery in the midst of life: the central fact we will experience without – we assume – knowing it. It is the stimulus to all other knowledge. Without it, there would be no sense of life, or 'life' would be something that is now incomprehensible.

Death is common yet to each of us as unique as the birth we cannot remember, and different from birth, which enables all we know. Nothing is more certain, and, for most of us, nothing more difficult to believe in as a personal fact, the 'state' in which we will no longer be.

Death incites poetry to eloquence, and is completely wordless.

Evening. Sue Gibbins drove over from Clevedon, bringing a beautiful bunch of freesias. I felt tired after the exertions of the day.

The bed next to me is now occupied by an amazing character. He is a Colonel, and says he is a Lord, and I hear him talking loudly and trying to flirt with the nurses. He tells stories: about pursuing a yeti; about his father being awarded The Order of the Golden Dragon by the Chinese; about his daughter who married beneath her – a gardener – and took her own life. All in a rich loud voice. He picked up a bug in Pakistan which gave him 'the squitters'.

11 August

This morning I took my first steps using sticks. Strangely, it brought back a memory of learning how to ride a bike – a little black one with rubber handle-grips like pipes – the alarming wobbling, the exhilaration of the first short unsupported ride, into, or in & out of, the garage at Fairacre. I suppose this was because riding a bike was the next big thing I learned to do after walking.

As I write, the TV is showing the Eclipse, with images of the sun from a Hercules aeroplane above the cloud cover, off Cornwall. Setting aside the science, there's a feeling of myth, as the sun is gradually consumed, as if by a wolf biting into it.

Later. I have seen the Eclipse, from the window beside my bed, through layers of cloud. Low grey cloud blowing across, obscuring the sun, revealing it – a scythe blade gradually brightening – through whitish cloud, a turbulence of blue & white, a shining edge. Landscape darkening; and outside the window a small spider stretching its legs, and suddenly running up its web.

Afternoon. A drive with Colin & Ros & Isobel to East Woodlands. Colin stopped the car by the church, St Katherine's, near the ancient oaks of Selwood. A stillness & a darkness, as though the after-effects of the Eclipse, were hanging about among the trees. Isobel collected small acorns in their cups, and communed with a tortoiseshell cat (like Marla) which walked along the church wall & the fence in front of the woods. Ros told me the oaks are diseased, and have been dying from the crowns since the hot weather of a few years ago. How terrible it would be if the oaks were to follow the elms.

I sat in the car and talked with Colin. He is a deeply considerate man, & reticent, not easy to know. He has opened to me more since my stroke. On a couple of occasions recently he has said things that made me conscious of my failure of sympathy & compassion.

12 August

Morning: a supervised walk with sticks round a path in the hospital grounds. Smell of the earth!

A nurse, Jane, seeing me writing, asks whether I am writing a book and says she will have to be on her best behaviour. I reply that I shall write nothing but good of her. Without payment? she says.

Afternoon: listening to a tape of William Carlos Williams reading his poems which Kim sent me. Williams in age, frequently making blunders (as he calls them) and starting again, at one point laughing at something that has occurred. A wonderfully good-humoured, human performance, as one would expect of WCW. His mind living in the poems – the man living, wry, sharp-witted, tender. Few poets in recent times have so used their poems to *think* as Williams did.

What a wonderful thing a truly new poetry is. In time we see how it connects with poetry that precedes it, and may even think there is only one poetry. But, no, it takes a particular human being to speak with the human voice.

I wonder if this is the reading Les wrote about.

'No defeat is made up entirely of defeat.'

Pop Mould, my grandfather, was a diabetic. I was aware of the fact (without knowing what it meant, except that he was ill), and associated it with the rusks he used to eat. He died at Canterbury House (Mother said he claimed May was praying him to death), in the upstairs room, where I was afraid to go.

Now that my medication has been increased in an attempt to regulate my blood sugar level, I feel ill for the first time since my stroke, in the late afternoon before supper.

Pip came again in the evening. I found myself talking to her about my intolerance, which I have become aware of in the hospital, as I have observed the opposite quality among nurses & others, and have had occasion to feel ashamed of rushing to judgement.

Colin came again later, & after Pip had left, we talked about Les, and agreed that our teaching was more fun in the past, when he was alive.

13 August

More walking with sticks – not exactly John Cowper Powys's 'Sacred', but serviceable. Practiced going up & down stairs, and found coming down difficult. Then another walk in the garden, noticing thyme on the lawns, and colourful cultivated flowers in the borders.

I have long thought I don't want to die in hospital, but would like to be outside, laid on the earth. Nothing I have experienced recently has altered this feeling, though I am now aware how unlikely one is to have a choice, when weak, in the hands of others, & subject to medical treatment.

Finished Holmes' biography of Coleridge with a choking feeling (literally, for at present emotion makes me choke not cry) – for the life of STC, & for the writer of this Life, who loves his subject.

Late afternoon. Home with M. after four weeks in hospital. In the front room, with my father's paintings, Lee's sculptures; lying on the bed where Mother lay. Now, for the first time, I feel the shadow of depression. Just tiredness perhaps. Or being where I expect to be well, and take for granted being able to do things, unlike in hospital, where illness is the norm.

14 August

Barry Cooper, the painter, very affectionate, came in in the morning. Among other things, we talked about Coleridge (he & Kath are about to go on holiday at Holford and he is reading *Biographia Literaria*). Also about an artist's or poet's embarrassment at his earlier work. It occurred to me (a self-reflection) that this could express vanity (appearing to disadvantage in the eyes of others), but Barry spoke of it as a positive thing, a discovery of humility, as in Pound's 'Pull down thy vanity'.

Day of brightness & shadows, tall clouds coming up from the west. Clear-cut vine leaves, part shadow part transparency, moving on the curtains.

Norman arrived late in the afternoon, on his way to Lindsay's 60th birthday party, returning later to spend the night.

In between talking & a few walks into the kitchen & garden, I felt tired.

Being in hospital brings one curiously close to strangers, yet without intimacy. Eric, for example, the big man in the bed across the ward, who was brought in after collapsing from a diabetic coma; Chris; the Colonel; Jack & Gwen, who died. It is physical intimacy – one becomes aware of their bodies & their conditions. Yet it is more than this also: something in speech, in facial expressions, the marks of the unique human being. At the same time, of course, hospital makes one acutely aware of one's own physicality – humiliatingly, though a sense of humiliation soon passes, there simply isn't room for it in one's mind.

15 August

Richard Kerridge, back from his OU Summer School at York, visited in the afternoon. He seemed appalled & fascinated by the drunken behaviour of a poet who came to read on the course. We talked with M. about the expression of emotion – English inhibitions, stoicism, boundaries, the demands of neurotic or distressed students. In theory, I take a hard line on these things – workshops are for the benefit of all; the educational experience shouldn't be sacrificed to one person's therapy. But of course, I am English! I don't like public displays of emotion.

16 August

Walked down the corridor holding my sticks but not using them. Sat at the table in the garden drinking coffee with M. under the birch-tree, which is shedding masses of seeds (tiny *fleur de lys* & little green phallic catkins). Green plums on the tall tree in a neighbouring garden. Slow-moving grey cloud opening into brighter cloud caverns – upside down airy caves.

Reading also David Abram's *The Spell of the Sensuous*, which I discussed with Richard. Very well written; but both of us have reservations. I'm sceptical of what I see as this new primitivism (updating Lévy-Bruhl's idea of a pre-logical participatory relationship between mankind and nature in face of environmental crisis), and am both drawn to the perception of the human within the web of nature and resistant to man-is-an-animal dogmatism, which negates the whole Western tradition of the rational soul. Richard met Abram in America and found him in his role of guru off-putting; also Richard thinks Abram simplifies Merleau-Ponty, whom he finds more obscure. I accept the thinking about participation (drawn to it by my own needs, as Lee is too), but feel the emphasis upon animal affinities (otherwise welcome) reduces human dualism or contrariety, our situation as (in David Jones's terms) 'borderers' between matter & spirit. There is also, in Abram & his fellow American thinkers, a tone of certainty that I don't like. As far as I'm concerned, the human is an open question.

Corrected the proofs of my paper on 'David Jones and the Matter of Wales'.

Evening visit from Philip & Zélie on their way back from a sculpture exhibition at Salisbury Cathedral. With deceptive casualness, Zélie slipped in the information that they are going to get married! Not long ago, Phil told me he had always thought it necessary to be completely independent, even in a relationship, and I had replied that I value nothing more than companionship. I feel he may have changed his view.

But of course, there isn't necessarily a contradiction between the views. I remember Mother talking to me about the place within, or inner self that is one's own alone, and can't be shared or communicated. How can we relate to one another if we aren't conscious of that, or don't value it?

17 August

> 'Subatomic quanta are now taken to be more primordial and "real" than the world we experience with our unaided senses. The living, feeling, and thinking organism is assumed to derive, somehow, from the mechanical body whose reflexes and "systems" have been measured and mapped, the living person now an epiphenomenon of the anatomized corpse.'
>
> David Abram

Practiced walking upstairs (the first few steps) with physiotherapists Ros & Janice, and walked across the road outside the house.

Daylong visit from Anne Cluysenaar. Anne (like all real poets, I would say) has a strong sense – albeit fleeting in its visitations – of life being different, *other*, from what it is generally assumed to be. This is the seeing that matters, in particular identities, but also as they are part of the whole.

It is my belief that many people know this – it is the human being's native gift – but we are surrounded by a totalitarian consciousness (only switch on the TV), which many English poets share, and it is therefore very difficult to realize a sense of the real *quick*. Even the word 'vision' is compromised, suggesting something rarefied, special, instead of perception of the world (as distinct from the advertised culture) we actually live in.

19 August

Lying here looking out of the window, I feel I could drink the blue of the sky, taste the snowfields of the clouds like ice on the tongue.

> 'As the experiential source of both psyche and spirit, it would seem that the air was once felt to be the very matter of awareness, the subtle body of the mind.'
> David Abram

I too have sometimes felt the 'sacred presence' of the air, with the concomitant sense that the self is an illusion, together with 'my thought': as though we all exist by virtue of the air – as we do – and by our participation in a common spirit, as we also derive our ideas from language & a common stream of thought. It isn't individuality I hold on to, for I can readily recognise it as a false idea produced by culture & economics. What I cannot resign is the unique person known in love. As for my own person, I can imagine death taking it away.

Western culture in the 20th century is a god that creates individuals in the image of death, encouraging each to think of himself or herself as separate, autonomous, though shaped by consumerist fashions & desires.

Afternoon visit from Lindsay, who brought James Simpson, the young poet whom I tutored on the MA. Lindsay's 60th birthday was an overwhelming experience. It included a 'This is Your Life' organized by his daughter, despite the fact that she recently discovered her mother, Lindsay's first wife, is dying from cancer. For Lindsay, there are three great 'participatory' experiences: in the womb before birth, at death, and through compassion.

Abram discusses Merleau-Ponty's use of the neurobiological term 'chiasm' (from ancient Gk. word meaning 'crisscross'), and speaks of 'the chiasm between the body and the earth, the reciprocal participation – between one's own flesh and the encompassing flesh of the world – that we commonly call perception'.

I find this idea, and Abram's thought & his interpretation of pheno-menology generally, suggestive. Its appeal to me is in its emphasis upon relationship, connection, the tissue that joins us to the earth & the non-human world. To my mind, however, Abram's treatment of nature and man-the-animal manifests a kind of innocence; or perhaps it is a deliberate reduction, made possible by the American idea of the wild, in which the human can be related directly to 'naked nature', without recourse to what my American online student Ramez calls 'Western civ'.

The simplification of the human as it has been interpreted and experienced in the West is accompanied by what I think is a sentimental view of oral, indigenous cultures, such as Native American or Australian Aboriginal. Indeed, this new primitivism is a version of Golden Age thinking, according to which the Western world took a wrong turning with the invention of the alphabet or the Neolithic Revolution.

Having said this, however, I greatly value the emphasis given to attention, perception, and the relation between the human and the non-human. This characterises poetic thinking, as I conceive of it; which is phenomenological (haptic or proprioceptive imagination working in the life-world), though usually more by instinct than theory.

This is not the enemy of a reasoning intelligence; great poets (e.g. William Blake) are supremely intelligent. We have no right ever to forget again the essentially humanizing virtue of rational powers, as experienced in their absence in the death camps, or that the greatest primitivist myth-maker of the 20th Century was Heinrich Himmler.

20 August

Pissed down my leg. A humiliating & uncomfortable start to the day.

Later I walked outside on the pavement, then went upstairs, twice, under Janice's supervision. A new vista: from Mieke's study, a view of the Mendips & Cranmore Tower. I was nervous of attempting this, and was encouraged to achieve it.

Morning visits from my friends Kath & Norman from Al-Anon. They brought me a flower in a pot & a basket of fruit, & a card signed by members of the group. I was very pleased to see them.

The flesh world takes on a special meaning for anyone experiencing physical debility. In hospital, shame soon goes, as a nurse administers an enema, and wipes one's backside. I remember one of the first things I heard from my bed in the RUH was an old man telling his neighbour, with passionate absorption & in graphic detail, about his bowel movements. And there is a pathos about others (as there is presumably about oneself) as one sees them helpless in bed, unable to control bodily functions.

This flesh, equalising, material, all of us certainly one body, but also each aware & suffering in his or her own way – and in this flesh, perhaps, a prayer for help or release.

In a hospital ward the notion of the soul is incredible. But its existence doesn't depend on credibility. In each face the person is most evident – and how believable is that in a world that is made of common flesh?

21 August

Outing with Emily & Jason to the White Horse at Bratton Camp. A warm, breezy day, with far views to a misty horizon, beyond the Mendips, Bradford-on-Avon, and the downs above Devizes.

Emily is full of purpose, working hard by driving a delivery van to make a living, and planning to take an Open University degree in psychology.

I find it easy to celebrate our vital sensuous being, but not to value it as an absolute, when I think of an old woman crying out to be allowed to die, or remember my own extreme physical weakness. Nature also is the earthquake which in recent days has killed or injured thousands of people in Turkey. It isn't only because of our failure to live on earth, in relation to other creatures & the elements we share with them, that we seek in & beyond ourselves for a power that is outside nature.

22 August

Hasty judgement (which I was guilty of) doesn't meet the case of Geoffrey Hill's *The Triumph of Love*.

A voice without a forum, speaking to itself about memories that should be shared, invoking a tradition to which those who should have inherited it are dead. Also (which is much the same thing) a poem about sin – which, astonishingly, at the end of *this* century, hardly anybody wants to own up to. But Hill does, exposing *his* vices, at the same time as he excoriates the loss of humanity (which means also recognition of our sinful nature) in a culture of 'savage torpor'.

It isn't a poem to *like*. It isn't, either, one that I can fully understand – in its references & learning; the *feelings* are palpable enough.

36

But is this how the English poetic & religious traditions end? Dryden, Milton, Blake, Wordsworth. 'Wesley, Newman, and George Bell'? Is this how *Europe* dies?

The temptation is to turn upon Hill, to mount an *ad hominem* attack. Who is this privileged academic exile to set up as poet-prophet lamenting & condemning the condition of the country he has left? Who is he, more than another, to show his feelings for the suffering of the Jews, or the dead of the world wars? By what right does he assume (does he?) a unique moral voice?

The questions are beside the point. Hill takes up his responsibility as a civic poet; he steps into the public arena which most poets have abandoned.

And still one doesn't have to like the result. Respect it, yes (as I initially failed to do). But that doesn't mean I have to accept it as the *ultimate* use of its poetic & religious traditions. For there is still life in them; they still contain a different life from that which Hill calls forth. It is in the understanding & interpretation of the human & the divine (the ground & the Ground of Being) that the traditions provide other streams of influence.

A poem may be '*a sad and angry consolation*' but that is not all poetry is for.

Later One thing Hill's poem is not – and this defines another reason for poetry – is an expression of gratitude for what he has been given. *The Triumph of Love* bespeaks a deep personal unhappiness, a bitterness of heart, as well as a cultural despair.

23 August

Climbed upstairs and slept in our bed for the first time since my stroke last night, and with some apprehension, since it reminded me of waking with that extreme weakness.

Thought for the Day on the radio this morning reminds me to look at W.E. Henley's 'Hospital Poems'. The blackness of the pit was something I glimpsed, but I was more aware of our ailing flesh than of the unconquerable soul. On the other hand I felt acutely the need for the courage Henley had.

Later in the morning I climbed both sets of stairs to my study. The books & writing on the desk, lying where I had left them as I was working on my paper for the conference, looked strange. Almost like things I had been concerned with in another dimension of time.

This perception soon passes, of course; but for me it has something of the quality of the creative moment, in which one sees into the essential strangeness of things.

24 August

Stiff-limbed after yesterday's exertions.

As I lie on the bed in the front room thinking of life at Hayford – often acutely feeling and seeing particular 'scenes' – I think of Mother, at the end of her life, lying in the same place thinking about her first home at Canterbury House, seeing the whole family grouped round the table, now that she was the last – and hearing the voice that said 'Start again'.

Nothing Mother ever said to me suggested she believed in death. To the last, she felt life in her bones. And now she is bodiless?

To ourselves & to one another we are inseparable from our life-worlds. At each instant we are everything that has made us; we are in the world we have made our own. But the eyes of love see *this person*, not a history.

When I think of death I think of losing the world.

> 'A clod of earth seems at first to be the embodiment of the stillness of death, but its apparent quiescence is completely illusory; physical, chemical and biological processes are ceaselessly active, bringing about continuous cycles of change, some upgrading, some downgrading, but buffered and saved from violence by the clay and organic matter. A steady balance is thus maintained so long as the soil conditions do not greatly alter…'
> Sir E. John Russell, *The World of the Soil*

25 August

Greenish-grey storm light. Thunder. Heavy fall of rain.

Lorraine drove Elizabeth Bewick over to see me. Elizabeth has been very ill in recent years – once, in hospital, she thought she would die, but, seeing that the doctors hadn't given up on her, decided she wouldn't give up either. She is strong-minded, this friend of mine; sometimes imperious & irascible (especially when she doesn't hear well), but warm-hearted, quick to enter into other people's feelings, and to help them with their problems when she can. Her sympathy was a refuge for me in the days when my marriage to Sue had broken down.

Why (apart from the difficulty I have in grasping even popularized new scientific theory) do I react coldly to Ervin Laszlo's idea of 'cosmic inter-connectedness', and a 'fifth field', in which every one – 'and all people and all living and nonliving things' – 'is a complex standing wave in a cosmic sea of invisible, but physically real, energy' (*The Whispering Pond*)? Is it because the theory itself is cold, without the love and fear invoked by the old unifying principle of God or Goddess? Humanly speaking, it seems to me, no scientific theory has anything to say about uniqueness – the lover and the loved.

26 August

Gillian Clarke phoned in the morning and we had a long talk. This was a voice I had been hoping to hear – she had only just learnt of my stroke.

My friendship with Gillian is dear to me.

In these past weeks there has been a kind of accounting. I have needed the support of family & friends, and have received it in abundance. The need has also been to know that my life has had meaning in the lives of others. Not that I expected to die, though I didn't – and don't – know; but somehow a conclusion (if to a phase of life) had been reached, and I needed to know I had lived to a purpose.

Clumsy words: it is love that one needs in one's weakness.

Standing in the garden in warm sunshine & a light, fresh breeze. Leaves shaking, wind animating clothes hanging on the line, as though, instead of our bodies, they were inhabited by spirits.

A few yellow leaves fallen from the birch-tree.

In childhood, and at times since, I have felt I could see life, or were on the verge of seeing it – a shimmering in the air, an almost visible body made of light & movement. Similarly, as a boy, I would sometimes see electricity flowing from a light bulb. Once, 'it' came to rest on the back of my hand, and was a brilliant blue-green fly, which startled and frightened me, and I shook it off.

Such moments (whatever they mean) seem to matter more – to go deeper into life – than years of book learning.

More commonly, I have felt pleasure in being – touch of sun & air on skin, smell of earth, life moving all round. It was the movement I had lost, and that was restored to me on Hambledon Hill, and in the field of wheat which was a golden waterfall. I never wholly lost it again, but before this stroke I had allowed it to become secondary, placing my studies first, and all the things that had to be done, one after another, in never-ending series.

I had forgotten that for me air on my skin is the breath of inspiration – not, primarily, knowledge of ground that comes from books, but soil crumbled in my fingers, wind moving in leaves, the sun that is everywhere, in everything.

Gillian suggested I write a poem about my stroke, called 'The Eclipse'. I don't know that I shall write any poem about the stroke. What I want to write now is a poem for my father.

> 'A true poet does not avoid influences or continuities but frequently nurtures them, and emphasizes them in every possible way ... Fear of influence, fear of dependence, is the fear – the affliction – of a savage, but not of culture, which is all continuity, all echo.'
> Joseph Brodsky, 'A hidden duet', *TLS*

27 August

Logically (as distinct from existentially – the shock of waking up in the night), I wasn't surprised by the stroke. On my 50th birthday I told myself – and I should have said the same thing (and acted on it) much earlier – that if I wanted to keep my health I would have to become much more physically active. But laziness prevailed.

I took physical robustness for granted – with an uneasy conscience. It was, I thought, an ancestral gift; even my brother David's early death didn't really shake my complacency. I thought of my grandfather, Thomas Alfred, vigorous in his 90s, of my father, enjoying his most creative years in his 70s & 80s; not wanting to dwell on their active lives, and different physiques.

I was like Dave telling stories about men still piloting aeroplanes in their 90s. In my case, a failure of commonsense.

Almost every day since he has been on holiday, Barry has sent me a letter – three arrived today – recording his walks, alone or with Kath, in the Quantocks (speculating about sites of *Lyrical Ballads* poems), along the north Somerset coast, and on Dartmoor. With his words comes a sense of the magic of West Country places – mud or shingle underfoot, fall of mist, tang of moist salt air.

> '…the characteristic of true thinking about living entities is that the observer actually enters into the object in an intuitive way; he lives it, he becomes it, he obtains an understanding of it (though this may be but partial) from the inside, in so far as the correspondence within himself is kindled into recognition. It is only through living in the fullest way that man is capable of apprehending the creative urge which has brought into being the mystery of physical life … In life we are in the presence of something which transcends the material form. Life leads us into the region of what has been vaguely named spirit; by thinking about life, rather than about things, we enter into the spiritual world.'
>
> E.L. Grant Watson, *The Mystery of Physical Life*

Late summer warmth, white butterflies twirling round one another. In the garden, my small domain enlarged by looking: clusters of bright red honeysuckle berries among holly leaves against the limestone wall; spiders waiting in webs on the rose of Sharon, and a number of snails, of different sizes & various colours (but predominantly leaf-green), which have climbed high onto the bush.

Multiple perspectives not mine – crumbs of dark soil, cloud blowing over.

When I become despondent at having few readers, I have to remember that, from early on, in *Soliloquies of Chalk Giant*, I was consciously writing poetry with a slow charge. Phil Pacey took up the word, in his *Charged Landscapes*, and I think it came from Paul Nash. At any rate, it was a word I was using then, by analogy with landscapes shaped by meanings that disclose themselves gradually, to the patient 'reader'. It was my feeling (as it was also my hope) that *Chalk Giant*, in individual poems & in the whole, contained a power that would thus reveal itself, and was quite different from the sensationalism that a sex and violence subject could easily display.

It was more than an analogy, perhaps, since in subsequent 'place' poems I was more aware of the hidden, shaping elements – boat-shaped mudbanks, for instance: historical materials, but also the feelings that charge place, human inscriptions ... Rather than being an imperious maker stamping my image on a personal landscape, I was aware of writing *in* places deeper in meanings than I (or anyone) could fathom. My hope, then, was to release charges, not merely to plant them, since the subject was one I was entering into – the life of a ground – not just a set of autobiographical impressions I was imposing upon it.

I don't say all this was worked out, then or now. I went to work with feelings, an attitude, and words like *charged* and *ground* expressed them, because the feelings were invested in those things, whether the blackened rib-cage of a boat in the mud of the Test estuary, or the broken 'mound' of West Wight, or Salisbury Plain.

Looking back, it doesn't seem I could have done other – and in that sense, whether it 'works' doesn't matter (though I hope it does). It seems to me, rather, that I have had something to give – and still do, in a new phase – and my business is the giving; one doesn't have any say in how – or whether – a gift is received.

28 August

Warmth & stillness under beech-trees near Alfred's Tower. Bright green starry mosses, crunching beech mast underfoot. We sat on the stump of a felled tree, our shadows sharp beside us.

Grey beech trunks soaring into foliage, domed-tree-shaped white clouds.

It seemed we could hear the rush of our blood in the silence.

My father is so *present* to me just now. Is annihilation more believable?

M. drove back on narrow twisting lanes via Brewham. I'm more than usually jumpy at present, starting violently at any car on a bend.

29 August

Jim is facing the threat of amputation. He rang in the morning. I had suggested recently we talk on the phone whenever he feels the need. He wants to *talk* (not about problems), and asks me to name a subject.

I mention my 'researches' into soil, the frustration of my ignorance of chemistry. What is alkali? Carbon? He talked for half an hour, explaining, drawing diagrams & pictures with words.

Reading in *Other: British and Irish Poetry Since 1970*. The rhetoric of 'marginalisation'. These non-mainstream poetries are now an alternative establishment.

> that chestnut sapling about to burst into leaf
> has more truth than I; burst of flame
> to be followed by green, flame reaching
> outwards and upwards, an offering of itself
> > John Riley

How few poets recognise the existence of nature outside their words. For many the verbal medium (whether or not seen in social or ideological terms) is all sufficient. Words that only relate to other words are lifeless.

30 August

E.L. Grant Watson quotes a writer (Russell W. Davenport) who claims:

> 'Abstraction has abstracted away all reality. It is possible
> to guess that in the interstices of the atom, as well as in
> the majestic infinitudes of intergalactic space, the physical
> sciences have come face to face with the spiritual without
> knowing what it is, or how to think about it at all'.

What a naive idea! Unthinkable in terms of the prevailing scientific wisdom. But only suppose that in those spaces, into which humans project their language & mathematics, divine creative power is at work.

Lunch in the garden on possibly the hottest day of the summer. Later, when it was cooler, we drove to Great Elm, and M. fed the ducks in the pool below the bridge. Bright berries on mountain ash. Blackberries ripening. Swallows on wires.

Moving about more, with more freedom on my sticks, leaves me feeling tired; the sort of tiredness that says 'Enough! This is where I sit or lie down'. Getting out of the car and walking across the bridge at Great Elm, among a party of visitors, I see myself self-consciously as 'disabled'.

> 'Anastomosis, branches forming sets, is a wonderfully onomatopoetic word. One can hear the fusing. The tree of life is a twisted, tangled, pulsing entity with roots and branches meeting underground and in midair to form eccentric new fruits and hybrids.'
>
> Lynn Margulis, *The Symbiotic Planet*

Jim rang in the afternoon. He goes to Portsmouth tomorrow to look at artificial limbs – he made a joke of it. Our subject today: The Periodic Table.

1 September

Tiny yellow snail sliding along a rose of Sharon leaf, sensitive dark horns waving. Coming to a stalk the snail crosses it, and begins to go under the adjoining leaf. Surely it will fall, but, no, it slides on under the leaf as securely as it had crossed the other.

Is it a coincidence that *all* the garden spiders (Grigson says they are also called diadem spiders), in their orb-webs, are turned away from the sun? Would it blind them if they faced it with *all* their eyes! I wonder if these spiders are survivors of the countless tiny ones – dots of gold dust – which we saw swarming on a single flower-head earlier in the year.

> 'Programmed death is a nonnegotiable consequence of the sexual mode of life. The great cycle in which males and females make sperm and ova with one set of chromosomes, only to have them come together again to make an offspring with two sets of chromosomes, is linked intimately with the imperative of individual plants and animals to die. …Evolution of the protocist [first established being] ancestors to plant and animal bodies required sacrifice and loss: multicellularity and complexification ushered in the aging and death of individual bodies. Death, the literal disintegration of the husk of the body, was the grim price exacted for meiotic [cell-fusing] sexuality. Complex

development in protocists and their animal and plant descendants led to the evolution of death as a kind of sexually transmitted disease.'

The Symbiotic Planet

Late afternoon: sitting at the end of the garden as the sun goes down behind the birch-tree. Wood-ash-white cloud in sky that has been blue all day. Swallows flying high. Two herb Robert, faded-pink faces, in the border near my feet.

Tired, my thoughts return to the past.

Dr Ellis called earlier. He confirmed what a doctor at the RUH had told me: that it can take years to recover 'completely' from a stroke such as I have had. He said I may never be as vigorous as I was. I have a sense now of the long effort before me.

2 September

Tony's birthday. He was excited and relieved when I spoke to him on the phone the other day. 'We're not rubbish.' He invoked Thomas Alfred as his model. Dad once said to Tony: 'we're good stock'.

This is 'the plateau' people warned me about, M. says: the point at which, having made progress I don't seem to be making any more. An illusion; but progress has slowed down. I walk with sticks, but don't seem to walk better. I sit in the garden (as I do now), and forget that only a short time ago it felt like a risky adventure getting here. I need patience more now than when I couldn't have got out of bed if I'd tried.

3 September

Evening light flooding the Mendips, whitening their outline; falling slantwise across my father's painting *The Avon at Ringwood*, in our spare room at the top of the house. Water illuminated, shadowed by a dark willow, brown with streaks of red, yellow, blue. Marks of brush and palette knife, like fingerings, thumbprints, and the name, *A. W. Hooker*, boldly inscribed in the bottom left hand corner of the canvas. The name which, in old age, he spoke with wonder, as though it had belonged to another man.

Rushes on the banks of the river, yellowy-green with a touch of blue, sappy as the common rushes Jefferies described.

4 September

How Tolstoy torments Ivan Iliych! But would Ivan have suffered less if he could have thought his life had been less false, and if he had been close to those around him? Most likely, Tolstoy is imagining his own death – and in doing so, enabling each of us to feel with him, or with Ivan, because the utter loneliness of ending is a common fear.

> 'Humans may be manifesting a particular form of behaviour in creative activity that shares basic dynamic properties with life in general, so that our creativity is essentially similar to the creativity that is the stuff of evolution.'
> Brian Goodwin, *How the Leopard Changed its Spots*

9 September

A lovely warm, breezy day. Afternoon outing to Shearwater with John Burke. We sat by the lake talking, oak trees at our backs, men fishing not far away on either side. Dark shapes of carp moving under the surface of the sunlit water, making ripples. A heron flapping over near the centre of the lake.

I walked 150 yards – John measured it – on the tarmac path.

Apart from this, I feel I may not be taking enough exercise. In the morning, when I have most energy, I like to read, with occasional excursions to my study (which are tiring) or down the garden. I need to push myself more in walking outside.

10 September

Recent days, following a very enjoyable visit from Kim Taplin have brought a supportive letter from Roland Mathias & a card from Stevie Davies, in which she speaks with love of my poetry. This is a wonderful coincidence: only last week I finished her novel, *Boy Blue*, and almost followed my impulse to write to her – an impulse I have felt, and postponed, after reading her critical books on Henry Vaughan and Emily Brontë.

It is impossible to overstate what such support means. It is confirmation, from a stranger whose work one admires. It brings with it recognition of a shared spirit, and is an incentive to go on, to take up one's pen and write!

Afternoon: sitting in the garden reading Jefferies's essays, in the book which belonged to my parents, in which I first discovered him. Occasionally a smell of fermenting fruit – plums are rotting in clusters on the tall, ivy-wreathed tree in the neighbouring garden behind me. A fresh breeze blows washing on the line, its shadows dancing over sunlit soil, leaves moving all ways on the birch in currents of air. Big soft clouds coming over from the west. Why do clouds never look shapeless? Instinctively, we recognise the 'chaos' in nature which scientists now analyse as law.

A croaking comes from under the bush or from a crevice in the wall at my back. When I stand up and look into the bush I almost put my eye on a beautiful full-bodied, heart-shaped spider, brown as a fresh chestnut and with cream-coloured spots on its back. Welcome to me but not to the insects drawn to the flowers where it has spun its web.

11 September

A visit from Emily & Jason on Saturday morning. After a game of scrabble with me, they took us out and bought us a meal at The Farmer's Arms, just outside Frome. Afterwards they did our shopping for us before driving home.

Glen Cavaliero, in his booklet on the Powys family, records that John Cowper, on his death bed, scrawled the word 'Alone' on his copy of Walt Whitman's poems. Of course we will never know what he meant by this, but I doubt that it had for him the desolating connotations it would have had for, say, Ivan Iliych, or had for me, in the state of mind in which, when I was alone & in fear of dying, I lay in the hospital bed.

Powys wrote with relish of aloneness, in which he (and characters like him) found the pleasure which there is in life itself. He carried this further than Wordsworth, beyond the 'joy' of non-human creatures, into the origins of life, into the organic nature we share with plants. In Mary Casey, with whom he shared much, 'Alone' takes on a different meaning, and is Plotinus's 'the flight of the alone to the Alone'; but perhaps it was also in her the Powysian death-acceptance & sharing in the life & death of nature (which we certainly do, however one may believe in an after-life).

12 September

When I read Jefferies's essays now, 45 years or more since I first read them, they are still more alive for me than anything I have ever read. Alive in the way of nature, as the drama of life occurs in the open air, the multitude of lives, the momentary changes & seasonal cycles, all (in Henry Vaughan's terms) the flying colours, and the quick as it escapes us. This isn't all there is in Jefferies, nor does he always *see* at his best. But for me, he works magic – in terms of a later theory he may well not have cared for, this Victorian sees phenomenologically: the actual magic of being in all its colours, rather than the light of ideas. Of course, he sought ideas, passionately; but in my view his genius was for poetic seeing (which knows its inadequacy to hold life), not for philosophising.

Blackberrying with M. in the woods near Gare Hill. Down a stony path, past yellow fleabane at the wood's entrance, past tall, fading valerian on both sides, and mare's tails. Dense woodland, slender oaks, birch, alder, ash, hazels on moist ground. I walked some way down the track until we came to brambles on either side. Sometimes I picked, sometimes sat on the folding chair M. had brought for me, while she reached into the bushes. Some berries were so ripe they fell off when we touched them, some were rotten, and the brambles were alive with insects.

At first, silence in the woods, one band of cloud like a frayed white rope, moving over. Then a robin came to look at us, perching on a bough. And soon there were several robins, chirping, twittering, flitting around, red breasts visible among green leaves. Noise in the understorey nearby – possibly a deer coming to drink at a stream.

Smell of crushed water mint on my fingers.

Bright coloured butterflies coming to the blackberries – a pair of commas, a red admiral.

Notes – steps - broken mosaics of light, where the sun shines through foliage, catching leaves, stems, bark. No order for the eye used to the mind's human ordering. Nature growing profusely according to its own laws. Looked at in this way, the woods are full of the ruins of our ideas of order – fragmentary pictures, broken images, scatterings of words. Perceived stillness becomes a trembling of light, on leaves & plants moving, carrying gleams of sunlight, losing them to shadow. Through leaf-work & branch-work and over all, blue sky, the rope of cloud replaced by soft puffs of cloud sailing over against the depth of blue.

Alongside healthy-looking, broad round alder leaves, some oaks had leaves brown-spotted with disease.

Earlier I had walked more than the length of Sunnyside, now, on the stony track, I walked farther than at any time since my stroke – carried by the pleasure of discovery, and a new-found strength & flexibility. Getting back under the wooden barrier barring vehicles from the woods was much more difficult!

If reality is magic, God is in the colours. Absence of colour is godless. Some people (M. for example) see the soul as colour: different colours/different souls. Not one Platonic Idea but a multitude of varied hues, any one soul being as indescribable as the colour of Jefferies's dandelion.

13 September

Two walks, with M. to the end of Sunnyside, where, in a paved area in front of the old people's bungalows and looking across the valley to the council estate on The Mount, there are a pollarded ash and a yew, with dead branches thrusting out of the living mass, which may have been there long before there were any houses on the site.

Is it a sign of returning vigour to start whining to M. about my neglect as a poet? In hospital, the feeling was too petty to entertain.

Merleau-Ponty, in his essay 'Cézanne's Doubt', reverses Pater's notion of the isolated, self-enclosed individual consciousness: 'the painter recaptures and converts into visible objects what would, without him, remain walled up in the separate life of each consciousness: the vibration of appearances which is the cradle of things. Only one emotion is possible for this painter – the feeling of strangeness – and only one lyricism – that of the continual rebirth of existence'.

Unlike Thoreau in America, Richard Jefferies, in the eyes of English metropolitan literary culture, is a minor provincial figure. There are aspects of Jefferies's writing (even in *The Story of My Heart*) that lend support to this view. In a European context, however, his iconoclastic attempt to see and think differently – the quality of his *perception*, which sees the life of nature anew – shares in the struggle of great painters and thinkers to penetrate below old habits of vision.

> 'Cézanne's or Balzac's artist [Frenhofer] is not satisfied to be a cultural animal but takes up culture from its inception and founds it anew: he speaks as the first man spoke and paints as if no one had ever painted before. What he expresses cannot, therefore, be the translation of a clearly defined thought, since such clear thoughts are those that have already been said within ourselves or by others.'

> '*The painter can do no more than construct an image; he must wait for this image to come to life for other people. When it does, the work of art will have united these separate lives; it will no longer exist in only one of them like a stubborn dream or a persistent delirium...*'
>
> Maurice Merleau-Ponty, 'Cézanne's Doubt'

14 September

Exercises at the Physiotherapy Department in the morning. I can now walk in the house, tentatively, using one stick.

In the evening, at my request, Mieke fetched up from the cellar damp copies of my school magazines, *The Stag* and *The Rock*, so that I could find my first pieces of writing, and work out how old I was when I first read Jefferies. The sentimentality appals – it is the embarrassment I spoke about with Barry – but there's a continuity also, in stopping to look and listen. What I have had repeatedly to break out of – for it is always tempting me back – is an idea of *sheltering* nature: country that exists for the sake of mood music & poetic reverie.

George Oppen, in his 'Daybook' (*The Germ*), wrote that Charles Tomlinson, 'for all that he is influenced by the Americans, and means to be, is a very English poet. More aware of "a peopled landscape". Less aware than we might be of the curvature of the earth'.

There, in a nutshell, is a major difference between English and American poetry of nature & landscape. I wonder, though, whether it applies universally. Langland writes of the folk & the soil & the Church, a ploughed land; Shakespeare, of the customary country. But what of Wordsworth on Snowden? Wherever he was, Wordsworth was always in his own mind, responding to nature, but at the same time controlling nature imaginatively. In each case, vision is held within the island: as Ivor Gurney sees the stars on Cotswold Edge.

The contrast is with Melville, Whitman, Robinson Jeffers, Oppen himself, who has a primary sense of the material planet, even in San Francisco or New York, as the rock juts out of Central Park. This sense moves me, powerfully, at the same time as I am aware that the American feeling for Wilderness can be as sentimental as 'Old England' nostalgia. That is, both can be equally selective as views of nature and history.

Les Arnold, from his years in Canada, had more of a sense of elemental space ('the curvature of the earth') than most English poets. I glimpsed something of it in Mynydd Bach. But I also saw the history of occupation. The same in the Wiltshire Downs, which have also commonly provided a sense of the oceanic, and of the planetary. The thing is – as Jefferies at his best shows – to see through or beyond one's seeing; to break through the pattern that the mind imposes, catching the eye of the wild creature, or becoming aware of energies and forces, which are as present in an acre of woodland as in a continent.

Looked at in this way, the how of our seeing is as important as the what. Thus, in England, with a surplus complacency that has survived the wealth & imperial grandeur on which it was founded, man the 'cultured animal' has remained content with a small range of ironies in respect of human existence, and a largely picturesque idea of nature. The result is an artistic coterie that is blind to art which embodies a new sense of natural energies, or when it is forced to recognise it (as in David Bomberg's paintings or Henry Moore's sculptures), marginalises or otherwise 'tames' it. There is a strong counterculture (which includes, among writers, Jefferies and John Cowper Powys), in which, for all the differences among individuals, nature as force and process shatters bourgeois ego-ideals & modes of perception.

I have come to think of this (with some influence from religious ideas) as a way of not knowing. Far from being a negation of perception, however, it carries seeing to its farthest reach. But the object is not to see within conventional frames, but to break them, by opening to the living world. My own need has arisen with a feeling of worn-out vision (and accompanying sensations of being blinded, choked, suffocated), from narrow concepts of the human, and a falsely pictured nature. Reading Jefferies again, and returning to the life flowing in my father's paintings, calls me back to the way I first glimpsed long ago – paradoxically in seeing that I don't see, knowing that I don't know.

17 September

Gerard phoned last night to ask after me. When I asked him how *he* was, he described himself as 'an old soldier fading away', who is taking one day at a time. He said he wished he could 'hurry it on'. (I remembered Lucy saying, sadly, it couldn't be hurried.) Gerard had been thinking about the parable of the return of the prodigal son, that it is addressed now to the Western world. I noted that he did not reply when I said twice that M. and I would visit him as soon as I was able to, and felt he did not expect to be there then.

A colder morning light falling on spiderlines between Lee's sculpture, *Clearing*, and the birch, on soil dark & moist after rain. On moving leaves & grass, that sense of windblown light, which I love.

Victor Turner sees 'communitas' in terms of Buber's I-Thou relationship. Communitas represents 'the desire for a total, unmediated relationship between person and person, a relationship which nevertheless does not submerge one in the other but safeguards their uniqueness in the very act of realizing their commonness'.

It is humanity that Turner is talking about, and for which he finds a plea in post-Renaissance individualist artists. 'The artist is not really alone, nor does he write, paint, or compose for posterity, but for living communitas.'

Turner finds in historical movements of iconoclasm 'the same human impulse to assert the contrary value to structure that distances and distinguishes man from man and man from absolute reality.' (*Drama, Fields, and Metaphors*)

18 September

Joe rang at lunchtime yesterday, from Below Bar, Southampton, where he is working as a sandwich board man ('very good with the public,' Emily says) advertising a computer cafe; for which he receives a little money, and free use of the internet. He was exhausted and feeling ill & unable to concentrate, as a result of his continual effort to come off all drugs. Should he go to his boss, explain his situation and ask to be allowed to pack in the work for the day, at the risk of losing the small (and now tedious) employment? We talked for a long time, but he reached no decision.

In the evening, I rang him. He still felt unwell, but had completed the afternoon's work (spending some of it in the pub). He is showing real resolution in his struggle to remain 'clean', and has been in frequent contact – for both our sakes – since being housed in Southampton.

M. talked to me about the change in herself as we lay in bed this morning. In concentrating attention on me since my stroke, and in her increased professional work, she has been able to let the past go, and live in every day, instead of thinking about the important position she once held, and feeling she had lost her place in the world. Only once in recent weeks did I suspect she had been drinking – it was when I was sleeping downstairs and she was ill, and I had the sick feeling which I had forgotten. It was a groundless suspicion, the very feeling was *my* illness (though probably an inevitable occurrence in the light of the past). Violent anger was part of it, and for a time, lying awake, I felt its poison in my veins.

Later Lee arrived at mid-day. He brought photographs of his new work.

Charcoal drawings based on tracings of tree shadows, 'like slices of the brain'. Sculptures which began in his thinking as 'stochastic sliced vertical'. Unnamed as yet, these are cellular structures retaining the mass of the oak from which they're carved. They have a sponge-like appearance; one of his students said, 'like the shape of thought'. Another sculptor said he had never seen anything like them – an ambiguous compliment.

Another step. Again, one can see where it comes from, but couldn't have foreseen it from the last step.

In reading David Bohm in particular, Lee has found a source of shared order in scientific writing. In his notebook he writes that so much of aesthetics 'seems concerned with notions of beauty and pleasure which I reject as being too limited, not what I work towards which is shaping states of embodied energy – powerful being'.

'an object is now considered to be more like a pattern of movement than like a solid separate thing that exists autonomously.'

'all has to be understood directly as relationship in undivided movement of the whole. In this movement there is NO THING.'

'We are the earth, because all our substance comes from the earth and goes back to it. It is a mistake to say it is an environment just surrounding us, because that would be like the brain regarding the rest of the body as part of its environment.'

'The whole is not imposed, but is *in* each part and each part is in the whole. That is what I call participation.'
David Bohm, *On Creativity*

At Bratton Camp in the afternoon: equinoctial wind at our backs, then in our faces, as we walked to a seat on the ridge by the White Horse. Hard going for me both ways. Cloud driving over, the whole sky moving, like a smokescreen beyond the lowland arable & pasture.

Drove back via Erlestoke & Devizes. Now & later, Lee worried at understanding 'romantic' (following John Williams's review of *Groundwork*). Lee feels that he is romantic, but is aware that it is a term of abuse on the current art scene, where it designates a soft-centredness & escapism from which he's keen to distance himself. (Not only because it could be used against him – and is – but because it is what he most wants to avoid.)

What does the word mean, then? The elemental, not the sentimental. Lee strives to get at the core of being – beyond knowledge – beyond ego. He went to live in the country in order to get away from the 'conglomerate ego' of the urban artistic scene, to face living in the world. He asked himself: 'what if I was making the first thing?' 'What would you want to body in the world out of your experience?'

He told me that through our first meeting & friendship, I had made him aware of the need for meaning. This surprised me, though on reflection I recognised our complementarity. He made me aware of the need to *act*: to work, to make images, instead of exhaustively studying and thinking. We both need to balance study and action. (In recent months, understandably, I have devoted myself entirely to reading and thinking.)

Lee brought a book about Enku, the 17th century Buddhist sculptor-priest, contemporary of Basho. In his youth, Enku had vowed to make 120,000 images. He may have done so, travelling among poor people in the remote mountain regions & fishing villages of Japan, working at speed, with his hatchet & flat file, mainly on cedar wood.

He made images of Buddha, images of Shinto gods, portraits; figures with magical power to protect people from misfortune.

His images of Kannon, for example: slender curved finger-like figures, simple as wooden clothes pegs, but with a grace in shoulder & listening head redolent of wisdom & compassion, or the complex, dynamic figure of thousand-armed, eleven-headed Kannon. Enku devoted thousands of carvings to Kannon. 'With solemn intensity he proceeds to break the traditional concepts. What emerges is a bodhisattva one wants to pick up and hug as a friend. There is an inner glow of genuine compassion, and it is easy to believe that Kannon forewent Nirvana to help humanity.' (Grisha F. Dotzenko)

Yakushi (Healing Buddha). The face is the essence of the benign, one would feel better simply by looking at it. And in this and other images, there is the illusion that the figure *looks back*, emitting benevolence, or wrath. This reciprocity is the magic of images. 'The metamorphosis of a chunk of wood into a living, vibrant being' – a being that responds to our response, or causes a response as a god or human being or other creature would. The image with presence speaks to us with embodied being; in its presence we become more alive.

By tradition, Enku died by 'voluntary mummification', buried alive, breathing through a bamboo tube and reciting the sutras, on the banks of the Nagara River.

19 September

Excursion with Lee into the Mendips. At Deer Leap, above Ebor Gorge, we walked on the grass and on the road – for me, slow, difficult progress. Below us, in a broad landscape, drama of light & dark, raincloud & cloud shadow over woods, hills (including Glastonbury Tor) outcropping from the plain, fields: a patched, blue-grey shadowy landscape, changing in changing light, dark clouds over whitish-grey clouds, rain. Rough-textured cloud in harmony with the land, swallows skimming dry-stone walls snaking along ridges.

We drove on in rain to Priddy & then to Ubley Warren, Charterhouse. Gruffy ground: an ancient worked landscape, mined by the Romans & by earlier 'groovers'. Gorse & decayed hogweed stalks among hummocks, mounds, gouged-out, grassy hollows. More like an ancient battlefield than places where actual battles have been fought. A bleakness like the lead mines of Cardiganshire but more overgrown. Dark red haws against dark rock.

I waited in the car while Lee explored, rain pouring down, streaming over the windscreen. We should then have stopped at a pub for a meal, but I had become anxious and felt off colour – partly at the thought of walking with difficulty into a strange place – and we drove home in a downpour.

Only a carved stick, only paint on canvas. But here a soul is portrayed, which activates in the beholder the powers of his soul. This also is what we mean by the expressive power of images.

Morning walk after early mist cleared – as far as the lime tree where the footpath past the old people's bungalows joins the pavement, near the bottom of Culver Hill. Moving quite slowly, head down, I see the other creeping things – slugs, snails, a small green caterpillar. Bright flowers in gardens – a white butterfly fluttering over the grass – Cley Hill & the Longleat woods in sunlight. A young starling whistles from the top of a tree. 'Juvenile,' I think, a word which, these days, sadly, automatically connects with 'delinquent'.

Have Christians wanted to hug Jesus, as Grisha F. Dotzenko says of Enku's Kannon? 'What a friend we have in Jesus.' But some of the mystics embrace him with over-heated sexual imagery. And the gospel figure has an austerity to be reverenced, not touched (except covertly by those seeking miracles). Gentle Jesus walks, too, in the shadow of his Father, and there is always a terrible threat for those who do not follow Him. I have felt the smiling face of Buddha denies seriousness – the tragic individual striving that I have learnt from my culture to value – but what I love in it now is the friendliness, without reserve of superior godhead, or menace.

The suffering figure on the cross, head bowed, sacrifices himself for Adam's sin. The question of sin is at the root of Western striving. Worth or waste: what is the goal of my life, what is the intention of every thought or action? What I do, what I am, has eternal consequence. Often, though, we are poor men & women (whether materially or not), in need of friendly reassurance or compassion, and perhaps too tired or discouraged to hope for anything but the peace of non-being.

But take a step further. The Buddha smiles on all, and we may interpret the solace as meaning 'Let go, detach, nothing matters'. But, as the priest said to Jim, 'Christ on the cross was thinking of *you*'. You are one of countless millions, but each is *thou*, you yourself, a unique person of infinite value. And, if so, inheriting the risk of infinite loss.

'The fear of death is not fortuitous, it is integrally bound up with our innermost essence, bound with indissoluble bonds: *This should be our starting-point* ... And only before great terror does the soul resolve to apply to itself that compulsion without which it could never raise itself up above the commonplace; the ugliness and agony of death make us forget everything, even our "self-evident truths", and force us to seek the new reality in those fields which seemed to us before to be peopled with shadows and ghosts.'

Lev Shestov, *In Job's Balances*

According to Louis J. Shein, Shestov, in adducing support for his faith that with God all things are possible, 'deliberately failed to acknowledge that the children that God "returned" to Job were not the ones who died, but were new children'.

'Lord, what fools these mortals be.'

22 September

Val & George Thatcher, on a visit from Ireland to their house at Marshfield, came over for lunch. George is 70, and is writing his autobiography in the form of letters to his grandson, or rather is writing letters, which Val is then typing up. She has been seriously ill; she lost a kidney after a bad fall when they were walking in Hong Kong, but she says she only gets more tired, which might be due to getting older anyway. She is my oldest friend from university days, and a deeply loving person.

I felt tired after they had gone, but was lifted by a visit from Phil and Zélie, who came to supper. Phil brought news of high drama in college: one of our most 'brilliant' students ever, who, having gained a first and signed on to a postgraduate course, had obtained a job at another college, has been discovered, retrospectively, to be a master plagiarist. Everyone who taught him and assessed his work was taken in. Tragedy for the young man. Embarrassment all round. The Director furious. I wasn't implicated (beyond having read a page or two of a 'brilliant' essay), but I can understand how such a thing could happen. Partly, it's a matter of mass hypnosis: student creates a good impression in seminars, produces work that deceives one or two people (who can't be expected to have read, or remembered, all the possible critical sources), and gains an unassailable reputation for excellence. But what will he do *now*? (Colleagues will be forced to adopt methods of impossible, foolproof vigilance.)

The day was a long, exciting one, full of lively & interesting talk; and at times I *felt* it, with the near exhaustion that overtakes me periodically now, but passes.

24 September

Occasionally, preoccupied, I stand up from a chair and, forgetting to pick up my sticks, walk a few yards without them, until my legs remind me.

This morning, walking with M. on a short circuit, to Long Ground and back, I was especially aware of lacking in strength & flexibility. It all depends on the comparison, of course: whether I am measuring my movements and stamina with how they were the day *before* the stroke (and all the thoughtless preceding years), or in the weeks *after*. The sensible way is to think about last week. But progress is slow, and as I lift up my feet, feeling the resistance of the pavement, frustration rises.

25 September

Bright yellow sumac leaves, shaped like long, slender arrowheads, lie on the paving outside the kitchen. At a glance, the yew seems to be standing in a reddish pool, surrounded by its fallen fruit. Nearby, clusters of black elderberries have weighed down their branches to rest on a garage roof.

Richard Bright came over for coffee in the morning. We talked about David Bohm, and Richard left me a copy of his own essay about the relation between art & physics.

In the afternoon, M. took me for a drive into the Mendips. Heavy rain, easing – floods of silver light falling through branches, shattered into shining drops. Rainbow below us, in open hill country. Then on the other side, as we drove back through Oakhill & along the Fosseway.

26 September

Two morning dreams: I am sitting in the living room, with my sticks beside me, at Brynbeidog. Alone in the house, I hear a noise upstairs. Then a big, magnificent tiger walks into the room. Thinking 'it must have escaped from Longleat', and fearful that it will attack me, I manage to push it out of the room with my stick. While closing one of the two open doors, it comes back in through the other. Having pushed it out again, I shut both doors, and take the phone from the windowsill and dial 999. But the dial doesn't work properly, and on three occasions I only manage to get muffled, confusing voices…

With no conscious transition, I am in the living room here, with my walking sticks, when Gavin & Richard come to the front door. I open the door with difficulty – there is a suitcase standing in the way – and, when they have come in, Richard congratulates me for having sold the house, for £82,000. But I love it, I say, pointing out of the window – at the garden of Brynbeidog.

Coming awake, I talk to M. about the dreams, and go over the past again, wondering (not for the first time) what I would have written if my life in Winchester had gone on as I expected it to. She tells me that I had to grow, which I know is true. For me, there's a sort of luxury in this kind of talk & speculation. My real life is with M., and every day, in a look, a word, a touch, I know how blessed I am.

Worked on my Jefferies lecture for several hours before and after lunch. In our walk, we went on the pavement by the road, past The Beehive, down Long Ground, and back past Sunnyside Place. The other day, I had turned back from this after only a few yards, daunted by the narrow pavement beside the road, and the long stretch downhill. It felt quite long, too, but today I made it. The fact that it was Sunday, with fewer people about, helped.

Tiny flowers of ivy-leaved toadflax on a wall. Sweet alyssum growing on another. Dandelion & plantain leaves sprouting out of tarmac, from the base of house walls. With all this limestone about, it wouldn't take long, if left alone by humans, for nature to heave up and cover it. White clouds piling up behind the wooded, Longleat hills. And soon the white clouds have gone, and masses of broken, grey & dark blue-grey cloud are coming over from the west.

29 September

More physiotherapy early in the week: practising to curtsey!

This morning, for the first time, I walked down Culver Hill and back on the path past the lime tree and Sunnyside Place. My left leg has more spring in it now, but I am aware that *both* legs are weaker & less flexible than I would like them to be. Patience, *patience*.

I am now back at the word-processor working on my Jefferies lecture. Judging by himself, Joe says this must be a wonderful thing for me. Well, it is good to be able to shape a rough draft, and to work for several hours before getting tired.

Reading again, John Skinner's *Journal of a Somerset Rector*, which I gave up after about 20 pages in hospital, because it depressed me. Even more than reading Jane Austen, this takes me into a different world. Where the parson, driven by a sense of responsibility, busied himself with everybody's morals, but especially those of the poor. It is hard not to feel for Skinner: he is such a driven, lonely, unhappy figure, heroic in his adherence to duty, and doomed. Like any revealed and examined life, it shows how we are all creatures of our time. And that itself is a cause of fellow feeling.

30 September

Walked the other way round the circuit, *down* Culver Hill, conscious of every unevenness in the pavement.

Awake in the night after dreaming of Brother Austen & Brother Oswald at St Peter's, I found myself reviewing what I have done with my life since then, and feeling how quickly the time had gone, and how poorly I had spent it. The point, I think, was a measuring against early ideals. Anyway, better than self-satisfaction.

1 October

Elin arrived from Amsterdam in the morning, after a very rough flight on the city-hopper.

Finished work on my lecture.

Some upset during the week when M., in a state of tension, took to drinking again. Not much, but for her a little is poison. I wondered whether this is something I simply have to accept, as one accepts the whole of a person one loves. In one sense, yes, because our lives are bound together until death. In another sense, no, because I cannot accept that she will damage herself. But I do realize the pressure she is under, with a sick husband she has to look after, and with the drain on her energy of caring for others.

My old French teacher, Brother Oswald, in particular, represents for me a man of complete integrity, kind & brave & strong. Instinctively, the words in my mind when I think of him are: 'he died in the faith', with the implication that he lived in it completely. Does this tell me that I harbour some guilt at not being a Christian/becoming a Catholic? Possibly. But as time passes I feel the impossibility. 'Faith' recedes, as something I once took for granted, when I was a boy and didn't know what it was, or that there was any alternative. Sometimes the idea of 'belonging' attracts me. But for the wrong reasons. From the position I have come to, I see the Faith as historical. The way I am on leads away – I don't know where.

> '…in actuality speech does not abide in man, but man takes his stand in speech and talks from there; so with every word and every spirit. Spirit is not in the I, but between *I* and *Thou*. It is not like the blood that circulates in you, but like the air in which you breathe.'
> Martin Buber, *I and Thou*

Buber's words, like Bonhoeffer's, ring with hard-won independent spiritual insight. But they have behind them a vast structure of authority, a structure that has the support of Moses on Sinai, Elijah harking to the still small voice: a tradition & a history, scholars bent over the scriptures in small rooms hidden in the depths of Europe, prayers of the faithful. And mostly, in our age (when a television executive describes soap operas as 'the soul of the nation') we feel all that has nothing to do with us, but happened long ago, in another universe, to other peoples, or else we simply know nothing about it. Or know, and feel the tradition as ruins behind us, or perhaps surviving in a man's voice, who speaks of 'spirit'. And there is in that now, without the great building overshadowing it, a loneliness…

2 October

We set out in the morning, M. driving us via Devizes & over the downs. Brown or whitish-brown, smooth tilth of ploughed fields, yellow stubble, cloud shadows. Past Silbury, barrows on high places, to Marlborough. Stopped for lunch at a pub at Ogbourne St Andrew. Arriving before I was due to give my talk to the Richard Jefferies Society, in The Village Hall, Liddington, we visited the small, compact church, All Saints, next to the Hall. From the graveyard, windblown shining grass-blades, yellow hawkbit, trees, a view of the long line of Liddington Hill with its embankment, cloud blown along & behind the hill. A place apparently hidden 'like an acorn in the grass', though we knew that, just out of sight, the M4 slices through the country which Jefferies knew, and the new conurbation of Swindon towers on & around the site of the old, small town.

I had a good-sized audience, among them, Kim & Jeremy, who had driven over from Oxford, and Roger Ebbatson, whom I met afterwards for the first time, and I spoke energetically for an hour, and then answered questions. I had put a lot into preparing this lecture, and it was important to me to give it, because I wanted to, as well as to fulfil my undertaking. I was anxious, naturally, but it went well. I had *done* it.

Back in fresh, late afternoon light, after rain. Mellow light on facets of the great stones at Avebury. Now, I was exhausted.

3 October

Joe with Maddy & Chlöe came for lunch, and Emily & Jason arrived afterwards, to see Elin during her short visit. While they talked together over the kitchen table, M. & I sat with Chlöe in the front room. She is an affectionate little girl. She surprised me by throwing her arms round my neck and kissing me, and the same with Mieke. I must say, it lifted my spirits – I still felt tired after the exertions of the previous day.

4 October

Colder. A bright planet in the dawn sky.

This would probably have been the day when I began teaching the MA again. Instead, as external examiner, I read scripts from the MA in Modern

Welsh Writing in English course at Swansea, and, perhaps inevitably, felt *hiraeth* for my years in Wales. Now, it is for that time of health, of course; although I also feel nostalgia for that situation in which writing mattered – and most of the writers the students discuss were my friends or acquaintances.

Ironically, only a very short time before my stroke, I was contemplating applying for a post in the department at UW, Swansea. Less from the desire to return to Wales than from the wish to work again in a university with a decent library. But the turn of events has underlined for me that I'm not likely to make any more professional moves.

How impossible it is to live entirely in the present. What would we be if we could? Without memory, or morals, or instinct – for that too must depend upon inheritance.

In Wales the Jefferies isolation would have been virtually unthinkable. Of course, a person could die of loneliness or despair anywhere. But in Wales, every writer, however solitary or hermetic, knows him or her self to be, in some degree, answerable. The writer's words always concern others, even when they don't read them. Indeed that is, often, the point: speaking for those who could not/cannot speak for themselves.

6 October

Another shining morning. Walked to the bottom of Culver Hill & back round the circuit. Frost lay on patches of mown grass but was melting. Fallen leaves crisply curled on paths. On the way back I walked some distance without sticks, but close to house walls which gave me confidence.

Continued writing letters in reply to the large number of cards & letters which I have received since the stroke.

Read further in John Skinner's *Journal*, deeply touched at the death of his daughter. The truly striking thing is Skinner's isolation, as a clergyman intent on doing his duty in a parish where he sees wickedness all round him, and perhaps from something unyielding in himself. In this world of farmers & coalminers, most of whom Skinner represents as malicious, drunken or dishonest, we are far from the benign world of Frances Kilvert. No point in comparing them – different men in different times – but it is impossible not to see the harsh contrast, which must have been due in part to Skinner's militancy.

7 October

After several days, work continues on the burnt-out carriages of the trains wrecked in the crash near Paddington, in which many passengers were incinerated in the ensuing diesel fire. They would have been preparing to alight, already anticipating the platform, the underground, another day's work. Whenever people have spoken of sudden death, I have always thought I would like time to prepare. But it is like a dream of control, of somehow easing one's way, advancing to the gates in full consciousness... But we have no *say*.

In our walk this morning we crossed the road – an anxious moment for me – and walked down Stevens Lane, where the old asylum used to be on the corner, and round through Lower Keyford, past the house which has a window of the medieval nunnery set in the wall. There is a curious story attaching to this place. Apparently, Ankarette Twynyho lived there. She was (or had been) lady-in-waiting to Isabel, Duchess of Clarence, and was suspected by the Duke of having poisoned his wife with 'a venomous drink of ale mixed with poison'. Seized from Keyford Manor House (XIIth day of April, 1477) by men accompanied by 'diverse riotous and ungoverned persons', assembled by George, Duke of Clarence, 'of his subtle conjected imagination', she was taken to Warwick, where she was hanged. This occurred eight months before Clarence was drowned in the butt of Malmsey wine. (J. White, 'The Old Nunnery, Keyford', *Frome Society Year Book* (Vol. 6, 1995-96.)

Today, the site of my unsteady but persistent steps. Impossible to imagine all that murderous activity except as a 'story'. Yet it happened, as sure as we walked past the fragment of the old nunnery today.

Another fun 'National Poetry Day', with 'loads of poets' (as a spokesperson for The Poetry Can said) given an airing in Bristol & elsewhere. Thinking of which, I read, in Robin Blaser: 'It is hell not to be in one's own time'. Yes. But how much sharing, and at what level, does it take to be in one's own time?

Late afternoon: to Heaven's Gate with John. Light slanting through beech trees, mist over distant hills, a soft breeze. Rook caws, rooks or crows chasing a buzzard, the bigger bird in a swirl of black birds.

I like the large ambitions of American (or Canadian) poets – Robin Blaser, say, or Robert Duncan: the creation of poetic forms that contain the making of a mind, a life. Do I have the nerve? I like 'cut' forms; I have perhaps a rather narrow idea of communication, which has prevented me from risking the kind of obscurity I find in Duncan. The irony in this is that I don't seem to be communicating very well anyway. Maybe I am still enamoured of the 'finished' product, yet dislike closure, little framings of personal experience, as Tony Conran would say. To what extent is the Blaser or Duncan ambition rooted in community? Even that of a few friends?

I need to risk more, not less.

8 October

Tired & irritable. I knock things over and lose my temper, shouting and cursing and banging my sticks on the floor. Mother used to speak of Dad 'flying off the handle', which *feels* like an apt description.

Returning from our walk this morning (round Lower Keyford & up Stevens Lane), we met John, the old Welshman, who recently cut the vine on the outer wall for us. In his eighties, John is asthmatic & arthritic, and walks with an aluminium stick. He said it takes him half an hour to walk the short distance to the shop for a newspaper & back. He was delighted to have been able to help us and enjoyed the work, which also got him out of his house. A man with a lovely smile.

Another dream of Brynbeidog involving Sue & a sexual rebuff. Again, the reading back. But why, after all this time, all the good years with M., should I still be haunted, and experience longing & regret? Is it the old desire for impossible completion, life as a series of perfect circles, which I perhaps derived from an idea of my parents' marriage?

Yet in this hyper-sensitivity lies, potentially, a life-killing inclination. This life, the life I have now, with M., is the life I want.

Late afternoon. This is the time when tiredness drags in me, like a force inside me – an emptiness – dragging me down. I feel it while talking to Mieke about the things I have written here, going over the past. A message in that.

But the past does come back, unstoppably. It is waiting within, in dark or twilight places in the mind, waiting for the sign that releases it. Last night Jim, on the phone, told me that Iris, his first girlfriend, has been to see him, and they talked easily and warmly together of old times. He reminded me of Boxing Day night 1959, 'under the stuffed bear': a drunken night in the roughest pub in Southampton – just now I can't recall its name – in which there was a huge stuffed bear in the bar. And he and Iris had arrived separately, and pretended they had got married…

And I was with Janet, but not with her, and hopelessly miserable, which happened a lot in those days.

Perhaps I shall gather these things one day. That's how I see the past. Not eidetically, as a continuous picture or series of pictures, but a sensation here & there, and as I dwell on it, images may come or a story begin to unfold. Self-pity tempts me, as it did my father, another romantic... But that isn't actually what I want.

I want the story or the song or the image: the human truth, whether in Homer, or ancient China, in my lifetime. It isn't in the feeling alone (which may lead to self-pity) or in the picture alone (which may be only circumstantial), but in feeling & picture together.

> To sing in ancient measures,
> to act as if harps still existed,
> where do people get the courage?
> And how do they still manage to speak of gods?
> Hasn't everything here become lonely?
> Yes, perhaps a whisper,
> one can do that,
> as if one spoke to oneself...
>
> Walter Bauer, trans. Christopher Middleton

10 October

Late afternoon, after sitting long over Sunday lunch with Barry & Kath. At East Woodlands. Clouded, quite still. Leaves falling occasionally in ones & twos. Acorns pattering down, knocking against leaf or branch. Yellow ferns, yellow & red beech leaves, among sombre greens & browns.

How natural it is for human beings, in woods or on rivers or in the mountains, to sense a presence, a spirit, and anticipate the ever-about-to-reveal itself. And one might die waiting to hear a voice other than nature's – harsh pheasant call, acorn falling. Behind all expectations perhaps the hunter listening. But don't assume only the material. What did the hunter also listen for beside the deer, what voices of the air?

Evening. A phone call from Jeff Wainwright. He had only just learnt of my stroke, from Gillian & Michael Symmons Roberts. We talked about *The Triumph of Love*, among other things. Jeff said it is a poem that doesn't expect to be liked, unlike practically everything else being written today. I think that's true.

12 October

Morning walk in bright sunlight. A drop of dew on the tip of every grass blade. Tortoiseshell cat on a bungalow roof (where it is every sunny morning) lifts a disdainful ear.

Thoughts on a Star-Map

For Lee on his fiftieth birthday

Venus bright
in the dawn sky
of your birth-month.

Jupiter and Saturn
crossing the sky
from east to west.

    Think of light
travelling for a million years,
more than a million,
the astronomers' unimaginable
numbers and times,
but light which the eye sees:

Andromeda,
sister galaxy,
faint as a smudge of dust.

    Think of the names
we pin on the sky. Imagine them
falling back like acid rain,
and the bright object,
without number or name,
swimming in its own light.

*

Time to begin.

A block of wood
lies on the studio floor –
a windthrown trunk
that was feathered with leaves.

New light flashes
through gaps in the roof
where lately swallows flew in,
cutting the air.

Think of the birds
flying away. Imagine the sound
of a human kiss
waved into space.
What will it find?
Who will know what we are?

Following our recent exchange of letters, Roy Fisher rang in the evening.
He had a stroke four years ago, and was more severely affected than I was.
He is still making progress.

13 October

Another shining day. Walked with M. to the post office & back home
via Long Ground in the morning. She then went out for the day, visiting
clients and I worked on the poem for my father, completing a first draft to
show her when she came home.

   Picturing, but to show what lies behind the visible, the life we cannot
see.

14 October

Completed 'Poem for my Father', adding one section & extending another.

A Poem for my Father

'The first region is colour.'
          H. W. Fawkner

November: a no-month grey sky
brings out the colours:
earth-red of a flowerpot in the garden,
brown soil and decaying leaves
washed fresh by rain.
The birch-tree is a yellow light
burning outside the window.

Inside, I pick over dead things:
a brush with stiff bristles,
tubes in an old paintbox,
battered and stained,
all magic gone except the names:
yellow ochre, burnt umber, cobalt blue...

*

Alkali or acid?
          It is knowledge
that dies with the man who knew soils,
expert on phosphate and nitrate, on mulch.
I see him in his old raincoat
fixing a garden line,
or treading down earth round the roots
of a young apple tree,
or pruning with a knife
curved like the horn of the moon.

He liked to say he came south
in a green winter, Yorkshire
edging his voice in the soft country.

We would hear him singing in the ward
as we came up the stairs –

death-knell of a fine baritone,
the romantic, handsome man
who liked women, single in his love.

Over his bed the painting of a cornfield
he could no longer see,
splashes of bright red,
bluish-green elms, the fullness
of summer days we could feel and smell.

*

It was fear also that he taught,
white-faced, his hand
electric in my hand – a man
hugging the wall by the stone steps,
following the hedge round the field,
crouching at the simultaneous
lightning bolt and thunder crack,
crying out,
    'Who should we help'.

  Fear and a pride
that might have been humility –
a man with Constable's
'God's gift of seeing', who avoided public view,
making his home his gallery.
   'A perfectionist,' he said,
'that's what I was' – an artist
who destroyed more pictures than he left,
who found a place out of his time,
and set up his easel by river
and in field corner
   painting
     impossible
       peace.

*

I have never seen a stranger thing
than his dead face,
false smile on an effigy,
an immaculate, dressed up corpse.

Outside, a downpour,
the streets of Christchurch
running with water,
the Avon racing full,
spray jetting from tyres,
leaves whirling or dancing
or plastered to the road.

I could think of nothing, only
a story he liked to tell – when
he was a young man working in Scotland,
one day, he did not go out in the boat
which was caught in a storm on the loch,
was not drowned with his two companions,
as his landlady thought,
who ran about the house crying,
'Wheer's my laddie, wheer's my bonnie laddie?'

*

Oak branches tufted with grass
mark the winter floods. On banks,
between leafless trees, yellow
of primroses, first daffodils.

In the stillness,
a woodpecker's hammer-notes vibrating.
From a wooden bridge, I scatter ash
which the current gathers,
bears down,
moving in snaking lines,
smudging dark water,
reflections of branch and sky.

*

I follow the way of the water with my mind
            flowing –
through wood and meadow,
under Boldre Bridge,
past the Shallows, where he painted
and I fished with my first bamboo,
the quick mirror-surface distorting us,
as here, it twists the trees.
            And for a time
all seems colourless,
until I look close and see again
the darkest dark that is depth
of colour – sky-and-water mix
of yellow and blue and brownish green,
the surface bark, or a nest of snakes
shedding their skins,
flicker-tongued adders of fire
dissolving in depth, the bodied
escaping appearances,
the bodiless the broken the whole
            flowing through.

*

It is the knowledge that dies,
stories one half-remembers
without the voice,
no particle of the living
reducible to an image or a word.

            In this region
there are no appearances,
no painted surfaces, only fire
that burns with the life in things.

To hold it
is like putting your fingers in a flame,
or trying to bring back an object
from a dream –

treading down firmly on the stairs of water,
rising slowly to the air.
And at the last something clutches
at your wrist and you wake scared,
hand tingling, your empty, open hand.

Later, following the physiotherapist's advice, I went shopping at Sainsbury's with M. Not too difficult, with a shopping trolley to steer (not unlike a zimmer!), though I was conscious of my legs, of course, and felt somewhat exposed under the bright, depthless lights. We had lunch afterwards in the supermarket cafeteria.

Jim & Caroline Dales came to tea in the afternoon. They are both lively, intelligent people, and Jim in particular is an amusing, quick-witted talker. He seems to be undergoing something of a crisis in his art at present, and perhaps with art generally, since he doesn't believe any work is being done which can stand comparison with great art of the past, towards which he has a humbling (and now inhibiting) reverence.

It seems to me Jim hasn't had the encouragement that every artist needs. Both he and Caroline feel acutely the absence of a responsible contemporary art criticism, a criticism that stands above the networking & hype, and has artistic values (which means also a sense of tradition). I agree strongly, but said that in the '60s (we are all of that generation) we rejected *all* authority, and may therefore bear some responsibility for the demise of critical standards.

But I don't know; on reflection it seems to me that what the art world lacks is truly independent minds, while the best of the '60s, after all, wasn't an automatic anti-authoritarianism, but a passion for independence & integrity. To this spirit, the commercialisation & conventionality of the present self-elected *avant garde* would have been anathema.

M. tells me that when she first saw me walking with a frame, in hospital, she cried: I looked like such an old man. I know she felt this for me. Now, sometimes, I feel older than I did before the stroke – stiffer limbed, quicker to feel drained of energy – but I am regaining strength, and have the chance to be stronger than I was. Not in body perhaps, but in using my life-energy.

15 October

Ernie Lowinger, my old schoolfriend, arrived in the evening on his beautiful, silver & black 1947 Vincent Rapide. Ernie belongs to a Vincent club; he stopped with us on his way to a rally in Devon.

Ernie is an emotional, highly intelligent man. He was born and brought up in Malta and his parents were Hungarian – at school, I recognised the difference that set him apart, and was probably the main cause of the abiding sense of inner loneliness, which he talked about now. He is an architectural computer consultant, and he has been very successful, working at one time with the architect Richard Rogers. But Ernie doesn't care enough for power & money & the social network to pursue success; he is evidently happier with his motorbike club and in consequence has not sustained the high life. We talked about the way in which some people – successful in these terms – live cocooned in their domestic & professional worlds, and don't need to reach out to others. We are both different, with need for friendship and an openness to it, (and I have been more fortunate than Ernie in sustaining close relationships).

16 October

To Toller Porcorum & the Kingscombe Centre in Dorset with M. on a mellow, misty morning. Sheep grazing on the Cerne Giant.

I received a warm welcome at the Centre, where we had lunch with colleagues & new students on the MA. Afterwards I held a reading/workshop with a group of about ten students. At the conclusion of my reading a young woman got up and walked out, saying I had said something that deeply upset her and she didn't like me or my poems. Apparently she had taken my comments on 'performance' poetry as a personal insult, whereas all I had said was that there are many different kinds of poetry today and this is mine – I am not a performance poet.

The episode shook me deeply, and I still feel it now. The other students were very warm and reassuring, asked me many questions, and each read a poem. But still I felt wounded and humiliated.

Why does such an incident cut so deep? There's the public embarrassment, of course; but there's also the thing in oneself that collaborates with the bad words. Ernie had talked about 'the dark side' of the mind, his own but also his idea of the poet's, and I had said that, while I knew what he meant and while I knew what depression was, I didn't feel that I had a dark side. Nor do I, if it means suppressed violence or malice; but I do have the inner voice which destroys all self-confidence. It is the voice that says 'he shot himself', since I was first depressed as a boy and thought about suicide. It speaks in my head when I feel embarrassed or humiliated, and sometimes when I have got 'above' myself.

In a way, such a response as the young woman's undermines everything I stand for. It negates me as a poet and all that means in my life. It also destroys the framework of mutual consideration & dialogue which I establish as a teacher. I could have wept! but didn't, though I couldn't conceal how shaken I was.

From the Kingscombe Centre we drove over Eggardon Hill & down to Bridport & West Bay, where we stayed at the Bridport Arms Hotel.

Evening walk on the beach. Golden Cap, the striated cliff like a giant mammoth tooth. Half moon brightening over the sea. Sea smell – salt & fishy on the pier, where people were strolling or fishing.

17 October

Dawn light through our sea-window. Long slow wave sounds on shingle. Then we could see the gulls, gliding, spiralling, *all eyes* for any edible scrap the sea might deliver. Gulls mewling, their piercing cries with a note as harsh as a donkey's bray.

This end of Chesil Beach (stretching from immediately below our hotel window) consists of countless tiny pebbles & sand, and the undulating surface is pocked with numerous small scoops or hollows, as though made by birds smoothing out nests with their breasts. What causes this?

Walking round the harbour on a fresh, breezy morning, we talked about our first things. For M., walking on sandy roads in Epse (Gelderland), the tarry, varnish smell of boats, the sound of water lapping against a hull, when she slept aboard with her family, near the waterline, on Friesian lakes. For me, bladderwrack, shingle, caved-in, concrete seawalls, gulls...

People were catching mackerel from the pier, rods bending & vibrating, silver fish thrashing in the air, on the ground ... Do I really *want* to fish again, as I thought I wanted to do, more than anything, in hospital, envisaging myself sitting on a rock fishing, somewhere in the

West Country? Probably I would become absorbed, tense with expectancy, as I used to be. It is the spectator who sees the pain, & the pathos.

From West Bay we drove to Plush, and had lunch in the garden at The Brace of Pheasants. It's strange that I don't feel romantic nostalgia here, and I don't think I ever have, while at one time I couldn't even have looked at a map of the area round Newcastle Emlyn. The truth is, I was still longing for Carol when I met Sue, and I wanted *to be married*, without thinking about the responsibility. I seem to have had little sense of the future then; living was all about *now*. And I knew even less about people than I do today.

From Plush to Mappowder, where we parked alongside the church and visited Theodore Powys's grave. And there, beside Theodore and Violet, Lucy Amelia Penny, with her dates, and the simple inscription:

Thank you

Gerard was sitting in his chair with the zimmer beside him. His legs, where we could see them between his trouser bottoms & thick socks, were terribly red & swollen. Mieke said afterwards that, this time, she could see no signs of health. Gerard talked about portraits of Katie (both in the room): one by Will, in which the eyes & face of the older woman are intensely expressive, and a much more professional one, of the younger Katie, by Gertrude, which is quite bland. Gerard does however have a striking painting of Durdle Door by Gertrude, which she gave to him & Mary as a wedding present. They had it on the wall of their house in Africa, and it was luminescent when the sun shone on it. (I imagined that it must have made Mary, in particular, long for Dorset.)

Talking about the photograph of a painting of Theodore led Gerard to talk about the man who called himself 'Count Potocki', who had stolen the original painting. Apparently Potocki had moved in with Violet after Theodore's death, and had caused no end of trouble. Gerard called him mad & bad; he had been a Mosley supporter, and he regretted Hitler's defeat, and said it was a pity Hitler hadn't had time to 'finish off the Jews'. Gerard blamed Louis Wilkinson for bringing Potocki to Mappowder. Louis, Gerard said, had a liking for 'extreme' characters.

Back at home, I rang Lee on the eve of his fiftieth birthday.

18 October

Seven years since my mother died. The only sign Mother gave that she knew she was going to die was on the last day, or perhaps the day before the last, when she quoted 'The plans of mice and men aft gang agley'. And extraordinarily, at the time, I took it for no more than one of her quotations, and responded as though that's what it was. How typical of her, though, to give no other sign.

Debbie Gregory & Lori Grey drove over from the Forest of Dean to see me, and Julie Rowell from Wiltshire. All writers who completed the MA, and have gone on writing, Debbie publishing her first novel earlier this year. A long afternoon of enjoyable, excited talk.

19 October

Bright light, cold wind from the east, more leaves falling from trees. Walked with M. to the post office and back round Long Ground.

Began taking notes on the books I have read in recent months, starting with Peter Ackroyd's *Blake*. I thought this good, but it impresses me more now I look at it again. Especially Ackroyd's sense of Blake's traditions, as when he describes what Joseph of Arimathea meant to Blake, or relates Blake's 'epiphany' in 'Pipe a song about a lamb' to Caedmon's messenger who requested him to 'sing me a song ... you shall sing to me'. 'So are the lives of the poets connected, and our English music is sustained by visions.' (I like Ackroyd's boldness, here & in his novel of that name, in affirming a tradition of 'English music', though the idea needs a good deal of qualifying.)

Started reading a PhD thesis on the work & life of Sidney Keyes.

After lunch I wrote 5 more pieces to complete 'From Debris', and, with them, I think, finished the new collection, 'Adamah'.

Ground-ivy

Hobnailed
imprinting the soil,
Adamah stops,
bound to the spot,

wondering at the tiny
smoke-blue flower
that bears his mother's name.

Originally, I was going to call the collection 'In Millennial Light' but when I mentioned it to Barry, I saw a shadow of disappointment cross his face. When I asked him why, he remarked, tactfully, that there are many current projects with the word 'millennial' in the title. On reflection, I realized he was right, and had politely shown me I was proposing to use a cliché. At a loss for a title, I came on the word *Adamah* in Abram's *The Spell of the Sensuous* and knew at once it was what I wanted.

21 October

Walked to Spar with M. on a damp, grey morning. Back via Lower Keyford, admiring the big stone walls.

Seeing the young diabetic specialist yesterday made me think. He was satisfied with my progress but I came away with an enhanced sense of the diabetic's 'vulnerability' to heart attack & stroke. I have good reason to know this, of course. But now, for the first time, I was thinking seriously that I might not live long, as I have always assumed. What an assumption it is! As though I knew nothing of the common condition. But what to do? Live each day, M. says. I can't quarrel with that.

Later I added four more pieces to 'From Debris', written in playful mood.

Enough now. If I were to go on at this point, I would overburden the sequence & the book.

M. brought drink in this morning. Coincidentally I was at the door when she came in, saw the bottle and took it from her. She thanked me, and said she had forgotten her promise. I don't doubt this is so; there is always a degree, more or less, of sleep-walking about her purchase of alcohol *and* drinking. We would agree in regarding a promise as a sacred trust, but addiction is an illness, not a moral failing (though I know how hard it is for anyone affected by a loved one's drinking to recognise this, and keep remembering it).

22 October

Took a new direction in our walk this morning, turning right at the bottom of Stevens Lane and coming back up Rossiters Hill. Slow progress makes me acutely aware of what we don't see, within a short distance of our door. But of course, we see according to our interests & preoccupations, and it's probably only a child or disabled person who notices – and values – the mundane details of an area.

I feel now, especially walking uphill, that my legs are wooden stilts.

During the rest of the day I began the slow work of preparing my chapter on J.C. Powys for 'Imagining Wales'.

23 October

Mieke in pain this morning, so I took my walk alone. Alternate bright light & shadow, wind & light rain. Low cloud like grey smoke blowing across masses of immaculate white cloud, openings on blue sky – which we see now, made familiar with it by photographs from space, as the planetary sky. Here, over council houses on The Mount (built over a medieval field system), over Cley Hill (shaped like a giant tumulus with a smaller one on top), over the Longleat woods & the hills above Warminster. The beeches behind the wall of Stonewall Manor are very beautiful now – yellow with a touch of gold among leaves that are still green. A few rooks were circling round their tops or coming to rest there. Swirling around the area a flock of agitated starlings – excited by some cause unknown to me.

I am aware that this is very much a social 'landscape', with the great house at Longleat hidden by higher ground, The Mount, where there is a good deal of unemployment, the old people's sheltered housing, the manor houses & larger stone buildings, in one of which we live. All within view where I take my morning walk, a social microcosm.

Later Jane Garbutt came to lunch, during which I realised Mieke had been drinking. Vodka & painkillers. Afterwards she went to lie down, and I talked to Jane, who said that, whatever M. might do, I had to live my own life/look after myself. I countered by saying that we are dependent upon one another. But I know Jane is right. It sounds like a hard doctrine, but in reality it is a simple truth: no one can live another person's life or should try. If I am not in & for myself, I do not live. If I do not live, I have nothing to give anyone else.

I poured the vodka down the sink. I should have brought the bottle out of hiding and placed it on the table. If M. must drink, she can do it openly. (Or perhaps not, because secrecy is part of the compulsion.)

24 October

Last night & this morning I have talked myself out again. If only M. would communicate, and resume the struggle, as she has done on several occasions, beginning with her stay at Clouds House. Her silence goads me to more desperate exhortation – always with fear of my own futility, and knowledge that only if she breaks out of her self-imprisonment (of which her silence is a sign) will there be hope. *I know that I don't have the answer.* But I can't stop trying to get through. It is her life and mine. If she goes on drinking, it will inevitably end badly – for her or me, for both of us.

This morning again, we were peaceful & companionable, walking to Spar & back in the rain, speculating about the reason for the great stone walls we admire – in the Middle Ages Keyford was, presumably, a small community of the wealthy, outside the more protected area of Frome, and within the outskirts of Selwood Forest, with all the possibilities of outlawry & theft. Hard to believe today, with suburban road systems, housing & supermarkets, but the surviving signs of another time are present in the bounding & protecting stone walls.

When I was a boy, bewildered by depression & guilt, and isolated within myself, I thought about suicide. For a time – nine months or a year, perhaps, at the end of my period at Rope Hill – I thought about it obsessively, telling myself that if I could get hold of a gun I would shoot myself. Of course there was almost no chance that I would get hold of a gun, especially as my mind was fixed on a revolver for some reason, rather than the kind of shotgun I might have been able to get access to (my friend Nick had one, with which he went shooting pigeons). Looking back, it seems most unlikely that I had any serious intention of killing myself. But the feeling was very strong – the isolating black misery inside me, which for a time was almost constant.

It was perhaps this experience, together with my strict – too strict – idea of self-control, that later made me hostile to 'confessional' verse, and especially to what I regarded as romantic attitudes towards suicide. (As well as reading the poets who wrote in emulation of Sylvia Plath, I knew students who identified with her.) Of course, I was afraid. That's not something I'm ashamed of. After my first depression, it was life that I wanted, even in periods of breakdown. Though I idolized several writers who had died young, the ones I wished to emulate were poets (Hardy and Yeats, for example) who had written in response to every phase of long lives. It wasn't that I wanted to write like any of them (though, even more than most young poets, I was a hero-worshipper) – it was the developing life-experience that I wanted to know, and to express.

Whether I have actually done this so far is another matter. Certainly I wrote the poetry of a young man – intensely romantic poetry – but, by the time I was publishing, I had already developed an antagonism to the confessional – or, at least, had discovered that I had no talent for it. How often I wanted to let go! In student days, when I was reading Ginsberg and the Beats; in Wales for a time, when I felt the appeal of Robert Lowell. But I couldn't follow either path – the poetry I actually had in me was different.

It seems to me that a lot of 'inner experience', offered as the subject of poetry, isn't interesting. For a start, it tends to be conventional, with more sameness (but less common depth) than its advocates are prepared to allow. The 'individual' is a bourgeois concept, a commercial asset in a society given to buying and selling 'lifestyle' products. The person, by contrast, turns away from convention, and instead of idolizing the psychological, as though it were precious private property, is sensitive to the unique and relational aspects of human being.

It is difficult enough for me to separate out the conventional in my own thinking and feeling. My poetry, when it works, discovers relationship, takes steps towards a greater understanding of how I, the human self, am situated – what I am made of (in David Jones's terms), and where I am 'placed'. It is a personal quest, whether I say 'I' or not. I am acutely conscious of being alive now, of being this person and no other, of loving these people and being drawn to these things. I may be too conscious of the personal, through my relative lack of a public space (as in this journal I can speak with more freedom than anywhere else), but my voice is, certainly, personal.

From the sameness of inner experience (as I see it) I was drawn in my earlier poetry to places & objects, and therefore to connections & relationships. Hence *Solent Shore*, for example: not only a book of impression & memory, also an opening to the world in that place. ('World' meaning all that world means, or all I am capable of apprehending of it: history, natural environment, community, family, person, the ties that bind…) I have sought to be true to this principle, which is as much desire as ideal. It has meant, ironically, making the uncommon, the unpopular. What I have refused is self in a vacuum, or self on the street where styles are bought and sold. This is the case, not a boast. I don't know whether it would have been better if I had followed a different way, either earlier or later, when at times I have found the very isolation I meant to avoid. Rightly or wrongly, I feel there wasn't much choice – such as my spirit is, so I write.

This seems a lonely way now. But it isn't really. There is a strong tradition of independent thinking, strong in the past and strong today. And it has been my great good fortune to know and love the spirit in others.

Later *Of course* I neither deny nor undervalue true inner experience, whether psychological or spiritual. I am only deeply sceptical of a great deal that is advertised as inner experience in contemporary western society. It seems to me that a lot of it is the product of fashion, internalised sexual convention, for instance, or self-image based on superficial myths. We are living through a widespread betrayal of the human – intellectually, by the academic theories that deny its existence, commercially, by the rule of assumed 'popular' culture. No area of life is immune to this betrayal, which has deeply corrupted every aspect of human behaviour. The personal as I understand it resists this betrayal, and manifests itself in authentic inner experience. The psychology of individualism as a selling line shares in the betrayal.

This view, I suppose, accounts for my iconoclasm, or that 'puritan' choice of words that are relatively free of marketplace connotations & poetic journalese. It makes me vulnerable to various charges (not least in part of my own mind), such as elitism, preciousness, or, indeed, Puritanism. I defend it (not as an absolute: a poet has to have a feeling for the inventiveness of language) on the grounds that it excludes clichés – of thought & feeling as well as language. The *letting go* I wanted, and still desire, is an imaginative & linguistic enrichment, not an orgy of soap opera expression.

25 October

First thing today, we returned to reading *The Twelve Steps*. M. said that for her alcohol is an obsession. The shadow was in her face after the weekend, but had cleared by the time we went out later.

Walking from the car park to the Physiotherapy Department at the Victoria Hospital I made long, flexible strides. Jo, the physiotherapist, was very encouraging; she said I am now moving my whole body. It was also the feeling of being close to M., and the fresh, bright autumn day, that made this Monday morning feel a good new start.

26 October

Another 'first' on a sunny morning: walking with the aid of only one stick.

27 October

Our wedding anniversary. In the evening M. talked a little, with difficulty, about her addiction. (She had been drinking in the middle of the day.) She could name her qualities, but somehow her feeling of being worthless (which speaks with her mother's and sister's voices) outweighs them. It is terribly hard for her to speak about herself, her inner life. The struggle shows physically, with long silences, tears, few words. I am convinced that in this alone lies hope of real resistance to her obsession: except in so far as they help her come to this point, all my words are useless.

But wouldn't it be better to let the subject rest? So far, periods of non-involvement & relative complacency (on my part anyway) have always ended/resulted? in drinking bouts. Can we fight obsession, then?

M. agreed readily to my suggestion that the bottle should be left out in the open. I undertook not to throw any more alcohol down the sink. (Deception & secrecy are integral to the drinking. Of course, leaving a bottle out doesn't mean that another won't be brought in, but it may help.)

Earlier in the day I had lost control of myself. I was also feeling contaminated by the woman who had walked out of my reading; apparently her grandfather had recently died of a stroke, and she blamed me for being alive. I knew she was sick, and I could see the situation impersonally, but I couldn't *not feel* it – as though someone had spat in my face. Unlike M., I can't deal with other people's mental sickness. I'm a teacher not a psychotherapist…

By the evening, I was calm. What I saw now was M.'s suffering, not its affect upon me. Sometimes I feel her drinking as a personal affront, especially when it seems defiant or oblivious to all else (as under the influence). But the truth is, I know and love her goodness, which is herself. And recognise her problem as my problem, whether or not she lets me in to share it – and when she does, I feel hope.

No, I'm not a healer, but I do know something about mental illness. For me, it means a long struggle towards wholeness. In M., I see how her very goodness relates to her lack of a sense of self-worth. (But do NOT accept that she cannot be herself without it.) If I knew more about the woman who wounded me, I might feel compassion towards her. That I don't, isn't *only* personal, because I feel strongly about anyone taking out their sickness on others.

At Aberystwyth, I flattered myself on being good with students who were stressed or disturbed. And perhaps, up to a point, I was – as far as listening and being kind and understanding go. But I couldn't possibly assess or even recognise real mental sickness, let alone give help. Yet as teachers we are sometimes confronted with it: it's my particular fear among 'creative writers', for whom shedding sicknesses (without being D.H. Lawrence) can be part of the process…

29 October

Blue tits in the birch-tree, yellow as leaves, blue as the sky seen between leaves.

The Third Step is the crux: 'Made a decision to turn our will and our lives over to the care of God *as we understand Him*'.

Naturally, M. strongly resists the idea of bowing before God (in whom she does not believe) or *any* Power. BUT she is a healer, and in touch with a great power. She will not *use* it for herself, however – it is the same resistance as that to advertising as a psychotherapist and to asking a proper fee for the work. She can only give with ease.

There is a thought-knot here, which I believe we have begun to unpick. First, she *does* have a sense of a Higher Power – stronger than most people's; she has been in touch with it all her life. Secondly, to draw upon it for herself is not to *use* it, in the sense of exploiting it for selfish ends, any more than we think of using food or air in that way.

One intellectual problem has been M.'s reaction against a narrow version of feminism – basically: leave-the-man-and-become-a-lesbian – which she has identified with the Movement as a whole. She met this among women in the Netherlands, and, as a woman who loves men, and a professional woman with a strong attachment and sense of responsibility to her family, reacted against it with anger. In consequence she also cut herself off from the very stream of thought & feeling about women's healing power of which she herself is living proof.

What I don't want is to become too schematic in theorising about this. Clearly the problem is not only intellectual. But it is that also – and I know *M's thinking* about it is helpful – I can see it in her face & whole body-language. My habit of working things out in my mind isn't helpful – only my part in dialogue is.

30 October

In Frome, we climbed the Church Steps to St John's, where we bought charity Christmas cards, as we do every year. Outside, wind was blowing leaves off the acacia, which whirled past us as we walked back down the Steps. It was making leaves dance and fly over the Safeway car park.

Despite the leaves in the air and on the ground, there are still many on the trees. Yet this morning I felt a new nakedness in the light when I first looked out of the window, possibly because of the wind-driven cloud, and in anticipation of winter, though now, with climate change, we can hardly expect a black – or white – winter.

> '…there come moments in all our lives, when, rending and tearing at the very roots of our own existence, we seek to extricate ourselves out of the way of ourselves, as if we were seeking to make room for some deeper personality within us which is ourself and yet not ourself. This is that impersonal element which the aesthetic sense demands in all supreme works of art so that the soul may find at once its realization of itself and its liberation from itself.'
> John Cowper Powys, *The Complex Vision*

31 October

Simon Millward came to lunch, on his way to see our old friend Brian Knowler, who is very ill. Simon said I looked 'more alive' than when he last saw me.

After lunch M. & I walked in the Longleat woods. Bright, windy day, quick-changing light & shadow. Golden beech-trees standing illuminated, gold & yellow ferns, oak leaves embrowned. We gathered white-fleshed, sweet chestnuts, leaves & prickly fruit falling in the vegetation around us.

1 November

Listened this morning to Jonathan Raban talking on the radio about his latest book. He spoke about the death of his father. Peter Raban was a good man; he tried hard to help when I was a troubled young man. I think he came to feel his parish, Pennington, was an apathetic and uncaring kind of place. That may have been why my parents fell out with him – he accused Dad of not doing anything for the church, or they interpreted something he said in that sense. Tony once suggested the real reason was jealousy, on account of Jonathan's success and my relative lack of it. (Tony warmed to Jonathan, because he wore a CND badge while serving behind the bar of a local pub.)

Over the years, I have had recurring dreams in which Jonathan has played a part. Perhaps these contain an element of emulation on my side, or Jonathan is one of the people to whom I feel I have to explain my life. This has everything to do with writing, of course. We were friends in our teens, and commented on each other's early writings. Later, we shared a cottage together when we taught at Aberystwyth. Our relationships with others put a lot of strain on our friendship, and afterwards we chose different courses – he went to UEA for a year, before becoming a full-time writer, I got married, stayed in Wales, and became involved with Anglo-Welsh literature.

It is a chronic insecurity on my part, this desire to explain. And perhaps it is really a need to justify, to myself but in the eyes of a successful writer. For me, Jonathan's path was the path not taken. Partly, because I lacked the nerve – in Bryan Johnson's view I simply didn't have the 'toughness' to make my way as a writer in London. But mainly because of my temperament and all that that implies – being the person I am, I opted for a kind of digging down. Certainly I wanted my way to succeed in worldly terms, which meant becoming known as a poet. But if I had known in 1967 what I know now about the making of poetic reputations in England, I doubt that I would have chosen a different way.

Yet the need recurs to know that it has been worthwhile; and this seems to require seeing one's lifework in other eyes. Not the eyes of a partial friend, despite the great value of friends' support. Rather in the light of a critical mind, critical and knowledgeable, both of one's own work and of literature.

I suppose this is why Jonathan plays a part in my dreams, despite the fact that we haven't met in many years, and most of our lives is unknown to each other. There is also the affection I once felt for him, and the interest to me of what he is making of his talent, which I recognised when we were both still schoolboys.

It is ultimately fatuous, though, this need for reassurance. There can be none except in the work itself, and then in one's involvement in it, the extent to which it is truly lifework – the thing one had to do, and which no one else could have done, so that it is signed by one's being.

2 November

My body is less like a badly wired, stiff wooden puppet now, but I kick out violently in my sleep, hitting Mieke. Last night was particularly bad and she hardly slept at all. Unless I wake myself up, I don't know that I'm doing it.

> 'If we do not attempt to discover the religious essence, the magic sense of things, we will do no more than add new sources of degradation to those already offered to the people of today, which are beyond number.'
> Joan Miró, in 1939

Michael Tucker (*Dreaming with Open Eyes*) contrasts 'the modernism of the socio-historical moment' with 'the modernism of post-Romantic primitivism, of the search for a healing language on the plane of cosmic religion'. Certainly John Cowper Powys belongs to the latter. In my chapter on Powys I shall be arguing, among other things, that as a poetic storyteller drawing on the world of the *Mabinogion*, he constructed Otherworld landscapes, marginal locations, in which the human imagination shapes (or conflicts with) 'reality'.

The role of the artist as shaman is peculiarly appropriate to Powys. Not least because he acknowledged the element of 'sham' or charlatanism in his play-acting. Herein too lies his modernity – he knew he was not the medicine man of a primitive tribe, but an alienated, sophisticated modern. Yet he made his magic work, as healing fiction.

When Tucker turns from painters to poets he excites my scepticism. The artwork as magical object, in, for example, Arp or Miro or Kandinsky, glows with numinous presence. What I am more aware of in modern shaman-poets, however, is pretension, the assumption of Blakean prophetic roles. It is Powys's humour at his own expense which, by contrast, validates his magic.

There is perhaps a disparity here between painted or sculpted image and verbal image. Is there still a residual magic about the former, or does it still draw upon sacred tradition, while the latter is imbued with secular consciousness? By his very peculiarities Powys reinvests symbols with magic (in Porius's encounter with the Cewri, for example). Powys creates the style and the story within which the Otherworld comes into being – it is the result of a tremendous imaginative effort, involving false starts (which include his actual poems, written in a dated manner).

Tucker doesn't mention Powys. For me, though, another effect of his book is to place Powys in the company of artists, in which he appears far less marginal than in that of most writers, whether modernist or not.

I am aware in this of going back over ground that I first visited nearly 30 years ago. The subject has great depth, however; and I feel that I understand it better now, because I have gone on studying it.

I have recently asked myself whether the stroke was a wake-up call. A call to change my life. Yes: in the sense that I can always be more awake, and awareness of death *quickens*. No: in the sense that I have work to do, and this is my way of doing it.

Lying in bed in hospital, I was aware of how much more I want to do, and thought that not to write the book of my collaboration with Lee would be my biggest failure. But I know too that it can't be forced. 'Imagining Wales' is also, for me, a necessary book. And this slow, patient working is my way.

This doesn't mean I can't see other things I should have done, and time wasted. But a time comes when to think of them is a waste of time.

Powys, like his beloved Whitman, was a cosmos. Still the voice I do not hear in him – and want to hear in my own writing – is the voice of the other, which comes from outside. His 'alone' may be a word of deep wisdom. But for me, being ill has only increased my horror of monologue, or at least, of a life that never breaks out of it.

'God cannot be an object of knowledge, because in the act of knowing man cannot rise above God.'
Nicolas Berdyaev

'Without something holy and precious carried over from childhood, one cannot even live.'
Feodor Dostoevsky

5 November

Outside the window, on a wet & windy day, the birch-tree is thrashing wildly – a fountain in a gale, green and yellow threads blown all ways. Glancing back at the book in front of me, I read: 'The shamanic tree of the world is most often the silver birch, the deciduous tree that is best resistant to the cold and that is most often found in the north'. (Jean Markale, *The Druids: Celtic Priests of Nature*).

As I walk up and downstairs, though more freely now, I feel as if I am dragging a weight behind me.

Earlier, rain pelted down, the country behind the tree and immediate roofs was whited out, reminding me of being in the caravan at Brynbeidog, on a small island in a sea of cloud or fog. Now the rain has stopped, the wind become gentle, and I can see the hills above Warminster & tiny lorries on the far road. It may be dry for Bonfire Night after all.

Dad used to say proudly that when he went for a job interview at the Ministry of Agriculture in 1945 and they asked him why he wanted the job, he replied: 'Because there is work to do'. That was a principle with him, and a need. I suppose I'm the same: the idea of a Golden Age in which no one needs to work has no appeal for me, and I instinctively make a strong connection between work and meaning, despite theoretic knowledge of wage slavery. The truth is that my experience of work, personally and in the family, has been, mainly, positive. And art is lifework, not an occupation from which one retires.

At present, I know I wouldn't have the energy to teach full-time. Sometimes in the day or night, I feel low in life-energy, a physical feeling of being drained or impotent, which at worst is deathly. This is close to the feeling of being helpless, at the mercy of other powers, which I have experienced perhaps three times in acute form – when Hans's yacht turned over and I came up underneath it, briefly entangled in the sail, when I had the car accident, and when I fell on the floor and couldn't get up, after the stroke. Most of the time now, things aren't as bad as this, and I study and exercise without becoming tired.

Later Tea with Jim & Caroline Dales at their home at Chapmanslade. Jim showed us his paintings in the studio & in the house. These are of two kinds: sensitive landscapes, which he describes as 'potboilers', and paintings of mythological subjects. The latter have a kind of stark intensity – contrasting, bright colours & sharply defined human or animal images. A recent series featuring the image of a cormorant, dark against darker sea, was inspired by hearing Tony Harrison read his Gulf War poems. The ones that impressed me most were of Ariadne, and the abduction of Ganymede, in which a terrifying, fire-red eagle with claw-like feathers, as well as talons, has seized the boy.

Over tea, Jim told us about the novel of the Impressionists he is writing. We talked again about artistic standards & values. About the difficulty of being a tutor in an Art School, for example, when student painters simply refuse to accept the criteria applied to their work. It is less difficult with creative writing, in my experience; easier to respond as a pluralist to the manifold differences among writings. But the situation with art in particular bothers me. The present chaos, in which a tiny self-generating élite publicize work which they regard at 'the cutting edge' – as in Turner Prize entries – and the wider public with an interest in art generally find emptily mannered or trivial. Of course, I have frankly to admit that I have a stake in this; but as one who cares for art, in the tradition of the struggle to make significant objects.

My critical work (as well as my poetry) has necessarily involved judgement, and has been an act of resistance to neglect of what I regard as valuable imaginative writings. But *passing over* is essentially the way of our literary and artistic élites, which pursue novelty (often, I would say, a dated idea of novelty), rather than interpreting the more demanding vision.

What can one legitimately do, though, instead of falling into blind fury, or demonizing others & deifying one's own judgement? Concentrate on the work in hand; show what one values, and why.

The appeal is personal, inevitably: the relationship one person forms with the work of another person. Neither subjective nor objective, but a response which reveals the grounds on which it is based. One can't write about a painting or poem without showing what one sees, and inviting others to share the perception.

7 November

Sunday. To Southampton, where we visited Joe at the house he shares with two other young men in Shirley. Afterwards, with Joe & Chlöe, we picked up Jim & Liz, and drove to a pub at Eling, where we had lunch. Walked by Bartley Water, brown between reed-beds, boats on mud at low tide on the Totton side of the bridge, and a small mountain of containers.

Mention of Watts Park as we were sitting over lunch brought up the subject of Isaac Watts & his hymns, which are also great poems. I could remember a line or two here and there – words I have loved since I was a boy – but Jim recited several entire hymns, and with feeling corresponding to the original. It's at moments like this that I realize the *life* of Christianity.

Jim has spoken to me on the phone about the likelihood that his leg will be amputated, but Liz told M. he doesn't want to talk about it. Today he walked over the bridge but wasn't able to walk back again.

Joe has been steadily reducing his medication – with unsettling results, but he has been doing it. He seems to be making good use of his knowledge of computers, and is taking a course at Southampton Institute.

Despite going over old ground, at Totton, at Northam, Cobden Bridge and the University, I had a rather dusty feeling about Southampton today. It wasn't that I was finding fault with the place but that my relationship to it seemed to belong to the past.

For so long I wanted so much to get back. But circumstances change and, with them, an idea of belonging fades. It is people to whom one belongs, and a phase of one's life which was shaped by shared experience. This is how I understand things now. My life is with M., my working existence is at the college; the idea of myself as 'a poet of place' had already foundered as a result of the Winchester experience.

It was a limited idea anyway, and I have rejected its narrowness. But I hold to what was best about it, in its passion for subject & relationship. Its main weakness, in my case, was the notion of an impossible support – that in living in a particular place a structure would be given. Now I know that the only way in my circumstances is the way I make.

9 November

A lovely mellow morning. In our walk, we went a little farther, round to Rossiter Hill and back by Long Ground. In Stevens Lane we stopped to talk to the man who is always sweeping up leaves or rubbish left lying on or beside the pavements across the road from us. Mieke complimented him on his work. 'Someone has to do it.' She said she expected it was appreciated. 'Not by everybody.' Then he told us about the woman who lived in the house behind where we were standing. Apparently she had told him to push off back up the hill and do his sweeping there. Clearly, this activity is a large part of his life. I noticed that, like Gerard when we last visited him, the man addressed all his remarks to Mieke and looked only at her, responding to her sympathetic interest.

Sometimes in our walks we talk about the future, wondering where we would like to live when I retire. We think about selling our books, moving into a small house, preferably near the sea. But we don't take anything for granted. I realise that, until I had the stroke, I had always thought about the future from a position of health – looking at job descriptions, for example, and assuming the strength to do the work, to move, to make a new life. The great difference now is that I can no longer make this assumption, and it is gradually altering my whole sense of things, especially as far as the future is concerned. We won't stop wondering and planning, but we both know that we have to live one day at a time.

Ita rang me last night. She had gone into college on the anniversary of Les's death, and met Richard, who told her about my illness. We talked about Les, remembering a wonderful period at the college. Ita, who is a devout Catholic, said, 'we are all going the same way, only some of us arrive sooner'. I know from previous conversations that she is totally convinced of the existence of an after-life, when we will all be reunited.

10 November

We went into the College last night to hear Tony Lopez read with the American poet David Bromige at the Tippett Centre. I sat rather uncomfortably on the edge of the audience not hearing very well. Both poets are intellectual and highly literary, and I would need to follow their poetry on the page to get the most out of it. I gave Tony the signed copy of W.S. Graham's *The White Threshold* which I bought on the Isle of Wight. I knew it would mean a great deal to him, and I have a copy of Graham's *Collected Poems*.

This was my first visit to College since July and I was glad that I made it.

Mieke got up early this morning and drank a bottle of white wine. She came back from her recent counselling session with Pippa with a new justification. Drinking is something she needs to do periodically in order to be not 'on call', to switch off from her responsibilities. Taking my morning walk alone, I found myself getting angrier and angrier. As if we weren't equal partners, and as if I hadn't carried the burden of her self-harm for the past few years, and even been made to feel, at times, responsible for carrying her life. And it infuriates me that she uses counselling to justify the very thing that is hurting her. It is also, of course, that I don't want to feel a burden or that everything she does, like driving to Southampton or taking me to the reading, she does *only* for me.

Again, she is in control; yet she has manipulated the counselling session, and found a reasonable and understandable justification for her addiction. But I am convinced the only way of overcoming it or, at least, *really* controlling it is by admitting powerlessness.

Alcohol induced oblivion, for someone who sleeps poorly and is in pain, may seem a reasonable periodic solution. But it is what it *does* over the long term, and the increased pain & sickness to which it is likely to lead.

Since lying in hospital I have thought that I would like to write something – call it a memoir or autobiographical sketch – about my childhood. Sometimes it has come to me as a memory of places, or people, or incidents. I doubt that I could do it formally, since it would confront me with problems of public persona & literary occasion – problems in my own mind about my 'rights' as an author.

What I might do, though, is give way to the impulse when it occurs, and use this journal space, in which I feel most free as a writer, to sketch a memory or an impression.

Just recently, for example, I have been looking at a blank – the transition from Fairacre to Hayford. I must have had feelings about leaving my first home, where I had spent the first seven years of my life, but I can't remember. The day must have come when, in the car (a grey Standard Flying 9: DOR 77, the only number plate I have ever been able to remember), with Dad driving, we left Warsash and drove through Southampton and across the New Forest to Pennington. But I don't remember it. I do however recall many memories from the years at Warsash, and I have vague memories of accompanying my parents to look at houses which they might buy, perhaps including Hayford.

What I do then recall is being there, in a virtually empty house, with cupboards to explore. And the garden, which then made a deeper impression on me than the house interior did: the row of fir trees – dense, dark green, with cave-like hollows under them – that shut off the garden from the neighbouring cow pasture, which I would come to know as Browning's Field, the tall firs in a corner at the far end of the garden, where we used to see green woodpeckers. (Once, one of them trapped itself in the greenhouse and Dad, seeing the bright colours, thought it an escaped parrot.) I recall also a square wooden post – splintery, dark-coloured: was it creosoted, perhaps? – which had been driven into the soil behind the garden shed – for what purpose, I never knew – and which held a curious fascination for me, probably because it seemed to dare me to climb onto it – which I did, and stood on the top, looking out.

The more I survey the place in memory, the more I see. The dense fir-trees, for example, become hiding places, and as I peer closer, I shall probably conjure up the companions with or from whom I hid there, in small caverns of naked branches & prickly needles. There is so much to find in and around the garden. Yet what I can't call back is the first journey, the last view of Fairacre, our red-brick bungalow in Greenaway Lane, the arrival at our new house. It must have happened, of course, or I wouldn't be sitting here now, staring at the blank! But what I recall is a host of first memories, from the later years of the war until I see myself standing on the gravel parking area, a few yards from Fairacre, just up Greenaway Lane – and perhaps then I was sad and anxious at the prospect of leaving? Then nothing, until I explore the bare floorboards, the empty cupboards and roomy space of the airing cupboard at Hayford, the house with an upstairs and a large garden, standing by the gravel track of Northover Road.

11 November

Window-views became particularly important to me when I was lying in a hospital bed. They were life-lines connecting me to the world in which people came and went about the business of daily living, walking or driving

94

cars, as though those were the easiest, most natural activities. Even when I could see no more than grass and a few flowers, a car park, trees and the sky, the sense of free living in space which these brought to me, was very dear. It is much the same now, when I am more mobile. Sitting at the wash basin to wash, I look out through the bathroom window, over a tangled area of branches and roofs and stone-walled gardens, which has the feel of an old Somerset orchard, and see in the distance the rounded form of Cley Hill. And it is the contrasts between near and far, and between entangled foreground and lucid distance, that brings an airiness, and free movement in space, into my mind. Or say, rather, my mind opens, shaking free of narrow confines.

I didn't need to have a stroke to know how wonderful it is to be alive. Yet it has accentuated the sense. Stepping out of the front door to take my morning walk, I am struck by the sheer rough *wallness* of the stone walls, the crumbly whitish fossil-printed limestone, and its contrast with the sky. Today, I wanted to call the sky *marbled*, because of the smooth, solid-looking blocks of cloud, with patches of blue sky between them. But even as the word came to me, I saw the clouds moving, slowly beginning to change shape – and realised the partiality of the image, of all words, which, in depicting an impression, make mental pictures that belie the reality.

I think it is awareness of death that has sensitized me to these things, not language but the actual *thereness* of the world. In a sense, all are given to being, and we take them for granted; they go with being alive. But death, which is unimaginable as non-being, forms, once one has come close to it, a kind of background to one's sense-impressions & thoughts. It is a largely unconscious process – a kind of placing of something dark behind the light by which one sees, behind the presence of walls and clouds.

The curious business of running away to see the world comes back to me vividly. More curious, because of the hermit existence which I later came to lead at Brynbeidog, strongly influenced by my agoraphobia. But it was *Gone to see the world* that I scribbled on the note which I left on my pillow, early one morning when I slipped out of the house and walked down to the shore at Warsash. Only the note *was* a scribble, since I hadn't yet learnt to write.

Why the shore? Did the world lie in that direction? I suppose it did. That was where we walked on the concrete sea-wall, eroded, with crevices and craters. Or on the shingle, with its windrow of old straw, corks, tarred feathers, grapefruit skulls, and wartime detritus. I remember helmets of

U.S. marines which had floated in, and tins of biscuits, which we were forbidden to touch in case they were booby-trapped. Most of all I liked the shapely, white cuttle-bones.

What I recall most from the morning of adventure was the physical urgency of needing to have a shit – the pressure on the sphincter, is that the word? I didn't know either word then. I remember, too, the humiliation – unless I have invented that. At any rate, it was accomplished, on a grassy bank, with no one around to see, and my bottom wiped with a handful of grass. I would like to say I remember running up and down the shore waving a bunch of seaweed – bladderwrack: how could I have forgotten it? I loved it as much as cuttle-bone – but it was probably the story I was told by my parents, who heard it from the two workmen who saw me and brought me home.

The second occasion contains a mystery. There was snow on the ground, and on the other side of the lane a snowman stood, with bits of coal for eyes. It was the snowman who said to me: *Go on, run away, see the world.* I heard the words clearly in my head. So I did, taking the path across the snowy field, and walking along Barnes Lane towards Sarisbury Green. About half way along the lane, between Warsash and the Southampton road, there was a wood, with tangles of barbed wire and a red DANGER notice strictly forbidding entry among leafless trees near the lane. I have always thought of myself as being a nervous, shy child, but because it was forbidden (as I had been made to understand, although I still couldn't read), I did enter, picking my way through the barbed wire, and walking into the ammunition dump. What happened then was that a troop of scouts, my brother Tony leading them, cycled past. He saw me, stopped, and with no more than a kind word, got me out of the wood and onto the cross-bar of his bike. His friends cycled on in the opposite direction, and he turned for home.

We had gone only a few yards when the bike skidded on the icy road, and we fell off. It was a hard fall, but my brother managed to save me from coming into contact with the gritty road. It wasn't until we were back at home that I noticed the blood covering his naked knee and running down onto the green tag at the top of his sock.

I loved and admired both my brothers, who were then ten and fifteen years older than me respectively. Later, talking about the privileges of my childhood, I would say it was like having three fathers. But I'm not sure that's true. I was a man before I came to appreciate my father. I can remember an element of dislike in my feeling towards him when I was a child. It was most intense, Oedipus-wise, when I was twelve or thirteen, yet I also recall, when I was a small boy, being offered his bristly chin to kiss, and hitting it… But I recall his stories too, his warmth, and his way of pinching my ear – a habit he had with those he loved.

But my feelings for my brothers were less complicated then, which I suppose is why I remember them better. They were both so big and strong: young men. (For a five year old, even the eight year old boys and girls seem formidably big and mature.) They were bold and brave, and could do things I couldn't dream of doing. For example, both would swim in the Hamble River, and dive down to the bottom, their white legs waving in the air, and come up clutching handfuls of gravel.

Both wore uniforms, too; they were part of their grown-up appearance. David was in the RAF, and had a blue cap and a badge. Once he went away to Jersey, and when he asked me what I would like him to bring back for me, I said a cow. And he brought me one: a toy black and white cow, which went with the model farmyard I won in a *Sunny Stories* painting competition, with a painting my father did.

Tony also had badges, and toggles, and a scout hat. He was a King's scout, a leader among men; he was strong, and kind, and never cried when he was hurt. I suppose that's where my passion of hero-worship began. From being a perfect scout, he became, as a young working man, when he was learning the craft of a carpenter, a communist activist, hostile to everything Baden Powell stood for. Yet he remained, too, a gentle man. I remember the scout hat, kicked into the corner of a cupboard at Hayford, where it remained, for me, an object to worship.

12 November

At lunchtime yesterday, after drinking in the morning, Mieke said: 'I find being very hard'.

We were back again with the old darkness and I was tempted to talk at her and at her, putting out all my powers of persuasion to drive back the shadow, and prove a fundamental love of life. Better, though, to let be, recognising the darkness not as absolute, but as a thread, a strand. So, later, in our warm loving, and in our walk today on another mellow, sunny morning, M. is happy to be alive. As I know she often is, without either of us having to say anything about it.

And this isn't to diminish her pain in living, pain of hyper-awareness of human suffering, as well as physical pain. It's to recognise how mixed her existence, or conscious life in any form, is, and to check my *hysterical* insistence on reasoning about human behaviour, and trying to force order upon it.

Anne Cluysenaar drove over from Gwent and spent the day with us.
 The voice of the male – a friend – saying to Anne: 'how can you possibly be interested in watching fish in a pond? They don't take any interest in you.' The same question about the natural world outside, as she stood looking out of a window. Are there really still people who think like that? Robert Minhinnick has rejected Anne's recent poems because they lack 'tension'. He doesn't appreciate the way of opening the mind to what is – *the way*, for it involves a formal and linguistic art every bit as demanding as a poetry of emotional conflict.
 Coincidentally, at the same time as I was watching the spiders on the rose of Sharon bush, Anne was fascinated by a large, beautiful, round-bodied spider among a patch of reeds on a field of her farm. But how write about it? How say anything new?

13 November

Colder. A ghost sun behind cloud. A thickening of the air, almost a feeling of snow, but not cold enough.
 We took a different route in our morning walk, turning right at The Beehive and walking down Locks Hill. Then along New Buildings Lane into New Buildings, one of the many interesting, hidden areas of Frome. Smaller, but massively solid stone houses in rows, but without uniformity. One, which was presumably the first to be built, has a plaque. Built by Robert Butcher (Gent) in 1814, on a two acre pasture called Elm Field belonging to Flintfield Farm. Mr Butcher would presumably have been one of the few near neighbours of the people who lived in School House (already Old School House?) then.
 Our immediate surroundings become more homely since we have been taking these walks. Sometimes we see the same few people, or exchange greetings with someone we haven't met before. We look for the tortoiseshell cat on the bungalow roof. (This morning it was in the road, looking malevolently at a dog, which was wagging its tail.) I get particular

pleasure at seeing the old yew tree standing in a paved area among modern bungalows. It was probably here before there were any buildings on the site, unless there was once a monastery on the ground now under our houses and gardens, as I have heard suggested.

I saw David less often than Tony over the years, and was therefore less close to him. But our feelings for each other were strong at different times, and quite strange. If anything human is strange.

I have pictures of him in my mind from periods in some cases many years apart. When I was a boy and he was a young man, for example, and we shared a bedroom at Hayford. Dad had bought him out of the RAF, and for some reason, this enflamed his anger against his eldest son. I say for some reason, but I can make a guess at it. There was the jealousy of a possessive man against his first-born, who drew some of his wife's attention away from him. There was also the question of nervous strain, of being highly strung, as we called it then. Mother had persuaded Dad to buy Dave out of the RAF because, otherwise, he would have 'a nervous breakdown'. And Dad, who suffered terribly from his nerves, was afraid of the condition, and dealt with it when he met it in others with anger or, later, denial. It seemed to be the only way he could control it in himself.

There were unhappy times in that period. Dave loved motorbikes and always had one, which he would regularly take to pieces, on the drive outside the kitchen window, and put together again inexpertly, sometimes leaving out a vital part. The impracticality, as Dad saw it, drove him into a rage. He would 'fly off the handle', as Mother said, or 'go off the deep end'. The commonplace metaphors, I now realise, were her ways of dealing with what was very painful for her. Once, when Dave was outside with his dismantled machine, Dad went for him, a wiry man, white-faced with irrational fury, out of control, flying at his bigger, stronger son. And Mother and I gripped him with our arms and, with difficulty, held him back. I can feel now the straining body, and the terror of grappling with a man mad with unreason, uncertain whether we could hold him. Afterwards, alone with me, Mother sat on the edge of the double bed in their bedroom, and cried, saying: 'I can't take any more, I can't take any more'.

Or did she cry? I'm not certain that I ever saw her cry. And I rarely saw her overcome by emotion. But on that occasion, she was.

One night at about that time Dave asked me to go for a walk with him. We walked in the dark up Ramley Road, past the field (I would come to know it as The Park) where Dave had been employed to pick turnips, by a farmer whom, from that time, he always referred to as 'P'und an acre'. It was a quiet night; there was little traffic on that road then. And in the starlit dark, I was startled to hear my brother's voice say, about our father: 'I hate him, you know, I hate him'.

The tragedy is, he would have loved him, even at the end, when Dave spent some time looking after him, in what proved to be the last year of his own life (he predeceased his father by five years), if only he had been shown love.

As I grew up, he came to seem younger than me, and he felt the same, and said so. He must have seen something in me that worried him. Once, at the beginning of a vacation, he came to fetch me home from university, in the sidecar of his motorbike, and took the opportunity, when we stopped for lunch in a pub, to warn me against taking life seriously. I think he knew what there was to be afraid of; he could have been like Dad emotionally, if he had let himself.

Dave did things that I was totally incapable of, like learn to fly an aeroplane, work in inhospitable climates to make money, in order to look after his family, and be able to afford his passion for flying. He only joined the RAF as an apprentice in order to be able to fly, but the war ended too soon, and his only future was as ground crew, so he was bought out, and eventually remade his life as a civil engineer. Yet there was something about him – a kind of innocence – that made me feel protective towards him. After a long period when we hadn't seen each other, he came with his wife and two young sons to stay with me and my wife in our cottage in the Welsh hill country. It was an area where low-flying jets practised, and everyone I knew feared and hated their sudden, violent and loud passage – come out of silence and gone again, leaving sheep and curlews crying in alarm, and children face down in garden or sandpit. But on this visit, at each thunderous interruption, Dave and his boys would run out into the garden, wild with excitement. If he had lived in such a place, it would have been because of the jets.

In what was to be the last year of his life, when we and our wives were taking turns looking after our parents, we came close to each other once again. On one occasion, we were lying together on Barton beach – he had been swimming, conjuring up for me the image of his white legs waving in the air, in the Hamble River almost fifty years ago. Now he was instructing me how to fly a plane in cloud, calling me Bloggs and issuing directions with an indulgent smile on his face, which I remembered from his RAF stories about kites and prangs and gremlins from the period after the war.

I asked him what he would do when he was too old to fly. He answered by telling me about a ninety year old man who was still flying.

Then my brother told me a story I had heard before, but whose details I had forgotten. When I was a fat-faced baby, he carried a photograph of me in his wallet. At Halton, where he was training, all the other RAF apprentices had photographs of their girlfriends, which they pinned up on a board in the mess. He had no girlfriend then, but he was very fond of me, so my photograph went up on the board. Sometime later, the apprentices moved camp, and the photographs disappeared. He felt the loss of my picture. About a year later, he was moved to another camp. In the mess there was, again, a board covered with pin-ups. Looking at it with idle curiosity, he was astonished and delighted to find my fat baby face smiling back.

The main reason I have never persisted in trying to write a novel – apart from lack of talent – is that I am haunted by what is uncapturable about people. So it is that, when writing about Dave, or my father, or anyone I have known, I glimpse a particular smile, or hear a characteristic phrase, and at once realise how little I in fact know. Not only of the person's inner life, but of their whole way of experiencing, and of the presence – utterly unique – which I loved about them. From the person, this extends to my whole apprehension of life, and my sense that words *always* distort or reduce it; in fact miss the very *quick*. I write poetry because, in it, I can break images and escape from categories – or try to – and express something of my feeling for that elusive quickness. But I cannot invent character, and in describing aspects of actual people, I am aware that they are only aspects. At times, when the whole family was together, I would become acutely conscious of the uniqueness of each one, and set myself to remember the sound of a voice, or to imprint on my mind the expression of a face; but afterwards, I was only aware of gaps in the air where each had been, and the absence of the unrepeatable, uniquely vital reality we had made by being together.

'It has become obvious to us now that every worm and midge and gnat among us is unique, though we cannot go so far as to say that we see them "as they are", for that theological-scientific illusion leads nowhere; and only implies that an attempt is being made to outrage and disfigure the very instrument upon which all our vision, limited as it may be, depends, namely the absolute subjectivity and individuality of the vision of things of every worm and midge and gnat and of every animal and of every man.'

John Cowper Powys, *In Spite Of*

14 November

Almost four months since I had the stroke. Progress is slow, but perceptible when I look back a week or two. This morning, for example, walking down Culver Hill and up the other side to Spar for a Sunday newspaper, then back through Lower Keyford and round by Rossiter Hill. Again, I used two sticks, and moved quite slowly, as though dragging a block of wood behind me. But I am no longer so aware of every unevenness in the pavement, or so apprehensive about crossing roads.

I have more energy now, too, and can read or write for several hours in the morning and afternoon. But I am still very jumpy, and emotionally volatile, as Anne said her husband Walt has been since his heart operation. I suppose the nervous system is more traumatized than normally appears on the surface. This morning, some kids threw a leafy twig over a high wooden fence; it fell on my shoulder, and for a moment I had to struggle to stop myself from shouting and shaking.

Fairacre was a small, red-brick bungalow built between the wars. But it really did have an acre of garden. My parents kept chickens and pigs, and after the war, I had a pig of my own, the runt of the litter, which we called Dolly. Her life story ended as all such stories do, and, although I was fond of her, I can't remember being deeply upset. The garden must have been difficult to cultivate – late in life, Dad described it to me as having 'as many weeds as there are devils in hell'. Even so, it wasn't enough for him, with his background in gardening which he shared with his father, who from boyhood had worked as a gardener on big country estates, and Dad rented another acre, at some distance up Greenaway Lane, and cultivated that too.

Dad eventually passed the field on to Tony's best friend. Brian was a young man we were all very fond of. One evening, after supper with us, riding the short way home, he lost control of his motorbike, either from a blackout or from swerving to miss something. He suffered concussion, and died in hospital. I remember lying in bed with a chesty cold, sticky and smelling the Vicks rubbed into me, and grieving. We all grieved, and Mother worried that something she'd given him to eat had caused him to blackout. But Tony was stricken. Sometime later, he came upon the motorbike, a Norton 600, leant against a kerb in Southampton, and wept.

On one side of the garden at Fairacre stretched strawberry fields, large flat expanses of gravelly soil, where, before the war – I have seen photographs of them – my grandmother and aunt and mother would pick fruit, kneeling between the rows – two beautiful young women, and a handsome older woman, all with handkerchiefs tied over their heads. This field belonged to Mr Pegrim, one of the local growers.

On the other side of Fairacre, separating our garden from that of our next door neighbour, there was a thick laurel hedge. Its mysterious density – anything might have been hiding inside it – and the shape of the leaves fascinated me.

Several hundred yards up the lane there was another laurel hedge. It started near a culvert, where the brook ran under the road, and followed the brook for a long way, leaving room between hedge and water for a path, which led to the second small school I attended, Miss Wemys's, to which, when I was six years of age, I walked every day.

We called this area, with the laurel hedge and the brook that really babbled, like the one described and pictured in the little blue-covered edition of Tennyson's poem, 'The Jungle'. Its greatest attractions were the running water and the laurel leaves, which I would pluck from the hedge and bend into the shape of boats, pushing the stem through the fleshy blade, and throw them into the brook, where they rapidly sailed out of sight, or were caught on some obstruction, and had to be poked free with a long stick.

The greatest terror of 'The Jungle' was a horrible bully called Gordon, an older boy who was the cousin of my best friend, Martin, a smaller and younger boy with whom I dug holes in the ditch outside Fairacre. Gordon would ride at me on his bike, fencing me in against the hedge with it, and menacing my ankles with its peddles. As with all bullies, there was always the fear of random and uncertain violence, that he would go too far, and I would be cast over the steep bank to fall on the stony bed of the brook.

My passion for justice probably dates from this time, for one day Martin and Gordon's grandmother, an old lady who lived across the road from us, and who until that moment I had always found kind, asked me, accusingly, why I and other boys bullied Gordon! I was dumbfounded, and stood looking at her, open-mouthed, which confirmed her suspicion.

A much more serious might-have-been is associated with The Jungle. One day when I was walking back on the path alone, a man stopped me. He was about Dave's age, and he claimed that he knew my brothers. He had an unshaved, bristle-bearded face, and a serious, even solemn, manner. He offered me a boiled sweet if I would do him a favour. What he wanted me to do was punch him on his bristly chin, which, bemused and embarrassed, but too polite to refuse, I did several times, but never hard enough for him. Then he asked me to step through a gap in the hedge with him, into the field behind, where he would take down his trousers and I would beat him on his bare bottom. He offered me more boiled sweets – a whole bagful – if I would do this. More bemused now, I also felt my inadequacy, for I hadn't been much good at hitting him in the face, and would be unlikely to fare better as far as the new request was concerned. Fortunately, the path was a public way, and although there was no one else around, I was able to blurt out an excuse and slip away home.

When I told my brothers about this peculiar episode, asking them who the man was who had claimed to know them, they took a very serious view of the matter, and made me understand that in no circumstances was I ever again to speak to strangers. The injunction bore fruit a few days later, when, walking home down Greenaway Lane, a lorry with two men in the front drew up alongside me and one of them started to ask me directions to some place or other. Which place I never knew, because, thoroughly frightened by the tone of my brothers' command, I took to my heels and ran home as fast as I could, bringing with me a look of amused surprise in the men's faces.

For me, the great freeze of 1947 will always be associated with the garden at Fairacre. The hen house was at that time infested with some especially large rats. My mother's father, whom we knew as Pop, reckoned himself to be an ingenious man, and in some respects, no doubt, he was. He was born in a thatched cottage in a village in Wiltshire, where, because the roof came down close to the ground, adders would get up into the thatch, giving him a lifelong fear of snakes. As a boy and a young man he had worked as an agricultural labourer, and had turned his foot over on a furrow, so that for the rest of his life he walked with a limp. One of his stories was about being in charge of a farmer's flock of sheep which he was driving down the hill at Stockbridge when he got them mixed up among the flock of another farmer, and so lost the job. Another was about being paid a silver sixpence for scaring rooks off a farmer's corn, and losing the coin in the field, and going back and finding it.

After an impoverished start in life, he had discovered in himself an aptitude for buying and selling, and for business generally. He had become a successful butcher at Park Gate, near Warsash, where my mother was born. He had made enough money to employ men to build houses – to this day there is one at Park Gate, with the initials HJM (Henry James Mould) incised in the brick wall near the eaves – and he kept cart-horses, which were requisitioned and sent to the Front during the First World War. There was still a stable at the back of Canterbury House when I was a boy, and I braved myself to explore its haunting emptiness – the space always dimly lit even on the brightest day by light falling through the cobwebbed windows, the mouldering harness hanging on the walls, and the powerful *absence* of horses. In fact, in all but one room, I was always afraid of something ghostly about Canterbury House. This could hardly have been to do with Pop, who, when I knew him, was an old man with a bald, shiny head and mild, blue eyes which always seemed on the point of laughing or crying. By then, he had lost his profitable business and kept a junk shop, in effect the front room – the one that I felt most at home in – which was full of decrepit, fascinating items, such as china ornaments that had been holiday gifts from seaside towns – *From Brighton With Luck or Love*, that kind of thing – old armchairs with jack-in-the-box springs rearing through the seats, and boxes of damp-warped books, novels, cookery books, copies of Gray's Anatomy.

Pop with his rheumy eyes was diabetic – a fact which was also to affect me much later. Mother loved him very much, and was deeply upset when one of her sisters, who had become involved with a married man and left home early, told her, many years later, when they were both old women, that he had not been good to *her*, and in any case he was a womaniser. I think my mother knew the latter anyway, and it didn't affect her feelings for her father, though it came as a considerable revelation to me. I realised that until then Pop had been a character to me, not a man.

At any rate, he devised a rat trap to help us rid our hen house of rats. This took the unlikely form of a piece of string arranged like a gallows over the hole in the hen house, where the rats came and went. Even to me, it didn't seem that anything would come of this. On one day of bitter cold, however, when hard-edged snow was stacked against the garden path, and lay like lumpy white iron on the soil, a day when all the men of the family were out, I went with Mother to feed the hens, and there was a huge rat – Mother called it a warrior rat – hanging in Pop's trap, with the string caught around his shoulder, alive, and glaring at us with baleful eyes. We were both afraid. After a while, though, Mother called on the help of the man who lived next door, who came with a spade; and so the rat died.

15 November

Gillian phoned again last night, rather mysteriously, to talk to me about a letter she has written to me, but not to divulge what it is about. But we had a long conversation about many things, and eventually she did tell me. An opportunity has arisen for her to sell manuscripts, including my letters to her, to the National Library of Wales, and she believes I will be approached to sell her letters to me. Reading my letters had made her vividly recollect the early years of our friendship, and what she generously refers to as the help I gave her with her poetry. I was also gratified to learn that she thinks they are good letters – well written – whereas my natural inclination to embarrassment would rather suggest a callow effusiveness.

Anyway, I have to admit that the prospect of making some money brings pleasure and relief. Of much deeper significance is the restoration of this friendship, together with the increasing confidence in myself *as a writer* that Gillian's enthusiasm has reinforced.

On a bright, almost cloudless morning, M. and I walked to the post office and past it, through Keyford, to Woodland Road. Here there are redbrick houses, possibly post-war council houses on the right, and, as the road descends, and becomes Summer Hill, a row of taller, stone-built Victorian houses on the left, each roof a little lower than that of the house alongside it, so that the houses appear to be descending the hill in steps. From Woodland Road the land to the east of Frome is visible, a quintessential Somerset landscape of hilly pasture and scattered woodland, and behind it the Wiltshire uplands, a plume of smoke from the cement works at Westbury, and downland ridges, long bare shoulders with beech crowns at intervals – the same I looked at out of the window beside my bed in the Victoria Hospital, and longed to walk over, on and on, under the sky.

Turning into Woodland Road from Keyford, I realised that the road we had just left would once have been a path through woods, the road we were on another one, branching off it; below, the early settlement of Frome, round St Aldhelm's church, and to the east, in what I was seeing as essential Somerset, further thick woods, with the chalk downs rising behind them.

This was one of our longest walks, and as we got to the bottom of Summer Hill and turned towards the equally steep climb up Locks Hill, I was feeling it in my legs. A short way up Locks Hill, however, we found a seat to sit on (driving past it several times a week for eight or nine years, I had never noticed it: one doesn't see such things until one needs them, and then they become major landmarks). This bears a silver metal plaque with the inscription:

> Erected in Memory of
> B.E. Wallis
> Cancer Patient
> For you to rest on.

And we did, gratefully.

After resting, we climbed to the top of the hill, by the traffic lights and The Beehive, and turned left into Sunnyside. This too is well named, like Summer Hill. In the morning, sun floods the garden and kitchen and my study, and in the afternoon and evening, the other side of the house is full in the sun. When I could first climb all the stairs again, though with difficulty, I climbed up to the spare room to look at Dad's paintings – two river scenes in particular – which we keep there. It was wonderful to see the paintings, his vivid sense of colour & movements of water & shadow, a vision of light, in the light that came in through the window, from the sun as it stood over the Mendips. Even now, as I recall it, realising how precious that sense is – life's colour, the human response to nature's creativity – I know how easy it is to lose it, as one settles back into a world taken for granted.

Although I don't remember which book it was (and no one is alive who could tell me) there was one story book which, when I was very young, I liked very much, and which I copied out, with absorbed slowness, before I could read properly. To this activity I ascribe the beginnings of something monkish in me, which manifests itself as scrupulous reading. In my criticism, I seldom use the first person singular, and although my critical writing, like everything human, is personal through and through, my aim is to interpret what is written, to illuminate and appreciate literary works, especially those which have been unjustly neglected. Thus, in writing criticism, my intention has been to report faithfully as a reader on the subject. The need to do so began, I think, when I religiously copied, letter by letter, the tale about some animal – was it a koala bear? – in a sixpenny book.

Actually, one of the two things I learnt to do at or before attending Miss Wemys's one-class day school – the two things that distinguished me from my classmates – was to read, silently or aloud, with remarkable fluency for my age. In later years, when the feeling of failure is upon me, I sometimes think this a disadvantage – a parallel to the copyist's instinct: the raising of a screen of written words between my mind and the world. I am not harbouring the idea of a simple-minded correspondence between words and things. I am thinking rather of freshness of sensations, including *hearing* speech, and originality of response, which is not mediated through written language. The discontent I feel at these times is perhaps a desire for a different kind of *slowness* – goodness knows I am slow enough in every other way – for a gradual absorption of impressions, on certain occasions, before the fluent reader's inner voice begins to turn its phrases.

The other thing I could do by the time I was attending Miss Wemys's was to draw Spitfires and Messerschmitts and stickmen descending on parachutes. Dave probably had something to do with this ability. During the war, he had been an expert plane-spotter, and there were balsa wood model planes (which Tony made. Dave, he said, had two left thumbs) and aircraft identification plans all over the house. As I have said, he joined the RAF because he wanted to be a pilot. The end of the war frustrated his ambition; he was made ground crew, without hope of ever being anything else; it hurt him deeply.

My war was even more of a romance. It is absurd to talk about it as 'my war', of course, but as I have seen the generation of the First World War dying out, and that of the Second changing from young men and women into old people, I have realised that, if I live long enough, the day will come when I will be among the last people with memories of the war. When I was an older boy, in the late forties and early fifties, I remember going for walks with a friend, when we would tell each other our war stories, embroidering or inventing some of them, for sure.

In consequence I can't be certain that I did actually see a German bomber, smoke pouring from it, going down behind trees at the edge of a Warsash field, or smell burning butter and see flames reddening the night sky, when Southampton Docks were bombed. I see and smell these things because I told my friend about them, but I can't be certain that I told him the truth.

My first real memory – it was my first memory of anything – was of being wrapped up in utility blankets – the feel of them, the smell – and being taken down into the Anderson shelter, where the whine of mosquitoes was sharp in my ear, and more actual than the crump of bombs which my parents and brothers certainly heard. Was I really shaken awake in my cot by the AA gun thumping in Pegrim's field? In these matters, the things one didn't experience, but was told about, are sometimes more vivid than the things one did.

Most terrific of true stories was my mother's. She was standing in the garden at Fairacre, holding me in her arms, when two Swordfish aeroplanes on training manoeuvres collided overhead. One of the stricken planes dived straight at her. She froze, she could no more move to save us than one of the apple trees could have pulled up its roots. The impact, which made the ground shake under her feet, was on the other side of the hedge, in Pegrim's field. My father ran to the crashed plane (the other had fallen somewhere out of sight); the pilot died in his arms. I knew nothing of any of this until I was old enough to be told the story.

Once, crossing Greenaway Lane to the smallholding belonging to the Binsteads, our friends who had been so supportive the year before I was born, when Tony had nearly died of meningitis, I looked up as I put my hand on the gate, and saw high up what looked like a vast formation of objects like crossed burnt matchsticks. Years later, I knew that I'd witnessed a thousand-bomber force setting out for Germany.

It was probably around this time that I went with my parents to a cinema in bomb-damaged Portsmouth. Then, it wasn't the newsreel of bombs falling, with a mesmerizing *waggling* motion that frightened me, but the tornado in *The Wizard of Oz*. For some reason, afterwards, as I lay in bed in the dark, I would be terrified of seeing the advancing toppling black chimney cloud.

Another thing I do remember, as sharply as the whine of the mosquitoes, was Dave carrying me out into the garden one night, onto the cinder path, and pointing up at the sky. He seemed to be indicating a star, bigger and brighter than the rest, which as I focused on it, broke into splinters of light – flakes of fire which fell in a shower like a rocket's, vanishing into the dark. This was a German bomber, shot down by guns on one of the ships at Pompey, as I was later told.

Remembering these tales now, I feel again the old temptation to indulge myself by telling more and more, all the true ones and the ones which might be true, as I did when I was nine or ten years old, walking up

Ramley Road with my friend Roger, on the way to look for birds' nests. I would have told him about the tanks that rumbled past, when Martin and I had been called indoors from digging holes in the ditch. Or I would have recalled visiting Southampton after the blitz, and finding what looked like gravel pits, but with fragments of wallpapered walls embedded in their sides. And whatever story I had told it would have meant the same thing: the romance of war which I, a boy untouched by its reality, enjoyed, and was able to relish, wrapped up in my happy childhood as securely as I had been cocooned in the utility blanket.

In my boyhood memories of an older war haunted the places I knew. In church, at evensong, I was fascinated by the brass plaques commemorating young men – officer sons of local gentry – who had fallen in the Great War. The pew we sat in was alongside these, and I would study them covertly, the illuminated names counterpointing the solemn words spoken from the pulpit. The Colonel was a familiar figure in the lanes in and around Pennington. Fishing at Wainsford, I would see him cycle over the bridge, a tall, gaunt figure in a dark suit, on an old-fashioned upright bicycle, muttering to himself, and occasionally speaking out loud. My friend's mother warned us that in no circumstances were we to make fun of him. Her words surprised me. I wouldn't have dreamed of doing so.

Later I was excited by war films and war comics and the gaudily violent covers of war books on station bookstalls. Later still, ashamed of being excited. As a man, I was affected retrospectively by the reality of that time, as much as anyone who hadn't experienced it could be. I was then deeply moved by reading Dietrich Bonhoeffer's 'Thoughts on the Baptism of D.W.R', written in the form of a letter to a nephew, born not long after I was. In the letter, Bonhoeffer says:

> It is your fortune to have parents who know by experience what it means to have a parental home in time of trouble. Amid the general impoverishment of culture you will find your parents' home a storehouse of spiritual values and a source of intellectual stimulation.

By the time I read these words I knew how lucky I had been. Far more discomforting were other words in the letter: 'you are learning from childhood that the world is controlled by forces against which reason is powerless'.

There's something in a person like Bonhoeffer which is hard to bear. It is the courage, and the goodness, and the evil provoked by those virtues to destroy the man, although he is not destroyed, for the integrity of his clear and courageous spirit lives on. And for me, in those words, it was the sense of my contrasting ignorance. I had known nothing about 'forces against which reason is powerless', in days when a cat scratch or a finger pinched in a collapsing deckchair was a major disaster, and I gathered my small treasury of tales on which to build my romance of the war.

What were Martin and I digging for? We might have said to reach Australia, but the real reason, surely was the love of digging, and our appetite for the look and feel and smell of the soil. There was an expectation, too, that we would find something – buried treasure, though it was satisfying enough baring a root or dislodging a stone. In the soil of the garden I found bits of clay pipes – fragments of stem, pieces of bowl – and once, in the gravel of a path, a perfect shepherd's crown.

In Woolworth's in Fareham, Mother bought me a book which probably influenced my imagination more than any other. It was a picture book, with few words: a history of life in Britain from the Stone Age (shaggy men and women chipping flints outside a cave) to the Second World War (a Spitfire doing a victory roll). Here was the past rendered in images: human beings wearing different clothes, doing various things at different times, in a changing landscape. Despite my fluency in reading, I had a feel for earth and stones. The craters in the bombed city drew me with their clays and gravels, as the smell of food would draw a hungry man. It was an appetite, fed also by the gravel pit in a field above the culvert in Greenaway Lane, where I waded timidly, bare-legged, wearing a white sun hat, among bulrushes – beautiful objects with long velvety heads – in the shallow pond. There might be worked flints among the gravel – and what else? Hadn't Roman galleys pushed their way up a local stream? In a Southampton museum, I saw lumps of mammoth tusks and stone tools, dredged from the mud during the making of the docks.

The Dump of wrecked German planes at Cowley, which I saw on a visit with my parents to an uncle and aunt, might have been prehistoric. I was ready for Paul Nash's vision, which I didn't see in his paintings until some years later, because I too had seen what he had seen: the frozen sea, the petrification of destroyed monsters, sinister but also beautiful in their death, with markings that hadn't faded – more exotic than the designs on moth or butterfly wings.

Prehistory was all around us in the south of England. It was in the mud and on the shingly shore; a bombed house might disclose it, or a crack in the pavement, or a hole in a ditch. It was the very chalk – the shining white sides of inland cliffs of West Wight, gleaming but charged with darkness, sea turned to rock, flesh to fossil. Barrows, as we called them, were things of great wonder then. If one thought about it, they made the idea of death beautiful, a home for the spirit in the breast of the earth. As for the chalk horse, what a wonder that was.

The one I first saw, from the back seat of the car, was on the way to Wiltshire, where my parents took me on visits to their friends. Ralph Devening was a gamekeeper, Connie was a warm-hearted Wiltshire woman, who was childless and loved children. She had wanted to adopt Tony – with his golden curls (before he cut them off in the bath) he was the most lovable of us, but he was that anyway, curls or no curls. I don't remember Connie wanting to adopt me, and to tell truth, apart from the encounter with the white horse, I don't remember much pleasure from those visits, which entailed going to bed with a candle in a strange room up a flight of wooden stairs, far from the comfort of adult voices.

Once, many years later, an academic colleague said to me, in a half friendly way, that he didn't believe in me, I was a character out of a Hardy novel. I took it in good part, I was even flattered (always depending on which character he had in mind!), but I didn't think the witticism showed much knowledge, either of me or Thomas Hardy. Had I told him the story about Ralph Devening and my father and a pig, however, he would have been even more sure of the accuracy of his remark.

My father had a fine singing voice, a rich baritone. He liked to tell people that when he was a young man living in Leeds he could have had a career singing with the D'Oyly Carte. I have souvenir programmes of Leeds Light Operatic Society productions of *Tina* and *Florodora* from the 1920s, and wonderfully staged photographs of my father, a handsome young man wearing white shoes and a white suit and holding a violin, or in bow-tie and striped smoking jacket, a reclining pasha surrounded by a bevy of adoring, muslined young women. I saw him, too, transformed, on stage in *Trial by Jury*, and watched enthralled, proud, and anxious for his success. As a young man, he had sung a selection of sea songs on the 'wireless'. (Do these survive in a recording somewhere, I wonder, or have they gone, as his comic and romantic songs have gone, and the hymns which, to my embarrassment, he would sing loudly at evensong in church?) At the very end of his life, when he was blind and immobile, he could still sing. It was the one thing he could do, he liked to remind us. Even the ruins of a trained voice have more music in them than the voices of groaners, which my brothers and I, taking after our mother in this respect, were. And, when I visited him in the nursing home, I would often hear one of the old songs being sung loudly and hoarsely as I climbed the stairs to the room in which, with other old people, not all of whom appreciated his 'noise', he was confined to his chair.

In the thirties, though, he was at the height of his powers. Then, when my parents with Ralph and Connie attended Calne Show, where there was a singing competition, Ralph confidently anticipated his friend's success. It was an agricultural show, and the prize for winning the singing competition was a young pig. To make matters more interesting, the competitors had to hold the pig while standing on the stage and singing two songs – one comic and one serious. If the pig wriggled out of their grasp they were disqualified. Such was Ralph's confidence in my father that he had made a wooden pen to take the pig home in, and brought it to the show. In the event, his confidence was well placed. My father may or may not have had the best singing voice of all the competitors – probably he had, and he made the audience laugh with his rendering of 'Young Tom of Devon', and moved them with 'There was a lady sweet and kind' – but he was certainly the one who knew how to hold a wriggling pig in his arms, and, without losing either it or his stage presence, *sing*.

16/17 November

Beautiful light over Salisbury Plain, as, M. driving, we set out on the journey to London. At first a sky of cloud-masonry, lilac, violet, grey, with broad rifts of pale blue; a great sky matching the Plain itself. Below, tank tracks, tumuli, a small Stonehenge, measured against the immensity surrounding it, but impressive too, from the angle at which we passed, with a few visitors dwarfed by the trilithons.

Today I was particularly aware of older Englands in place names and the remnants of former landscapes. The Bustard Inn on the Plain, a signpost to Broad Oak, the boy William Cobbett, playing or working, as we drove through Farnham, numerous parishes, reminiscent of Gilbert White's Selborne. In stretches of road, too, I was aware of my own earlier journeys, driving or hitchhiking to or from London as a student, with Penny at the end of an Aldermaston march, for example, or with Sue and the children, as we crossed Wiltshire on journeys between Wales and Sussex. And the roads we were taking now were older roads, because in the present state of my nerves, Mieke had planned a route avoiding motorways.

But even in the country one couldn't conjure up an older England, even if one wanted to, as Edward Thomas did before the First World War. Everywhere, noise of traffic, smell of petrol fumes, modern communications, marks which the sheer mass of us make.

By the time we stopped for a break, at a Little Chef between Farnham and Guildford, the sky was heavily clouded. And as we sat over our tea and snack, a hailstorm passed over, briefly enveloping us, and leaving a ragged pattern of hail, like frost marks, at the base of the windows.

From Guildford across country on winding roads in the dark. Into London & traffic, through many communities, no longer new, of course, but the homes of many different peoples; only 'new' to someone bringing literary ideas from another age.

In Greenwich, we booked into our hotel, and, after a meal, Mieke (tired from driving) had a bath and went to bed, and I took a taxi to Old Woolwich Road to see Julian May. It should have been a quick journey, but road works & an accident ahead made it take longer. Long enough for the taxi driver to tell me a story his father had told him. Henry VIII used to hunt in the woods at Shooters Hill, and one day he encountered 600 men armed with bows and arrows and all dressed in green. 'Robin Hood and his men,' the young man said, half believing.

Julian was at home, looking after his two young sons who were in bed asleep, while Sarah (who came in later) was out on an assignment, reviewing experimental theatre at Hammersmith. We sat in the front room, with its pleasing bare floorboards and wood panelling, and talked. Julian told me that he is not writing poetry at present, partly because, with his family & pressure of work at the BBC, there isn't time, but also partly because he doubts whether he is good enough. This was characteristically modest, and might be, as I remarked, Robert Graves's 'true poet's necessary sense of failure'. But there's also the truth of Saunders Lewis's statement that a poet is someone who has 'the habit of poetry'.

After Sarah had come in and we had talked together, Julian drove me back to the hotel. Through a gap between the houses opposite, I glimpsed Canary Wharf, like an illuminated, sugary confection.

The following morning John Williams called for us, and drove me (with M. following in our car) to Riverside Building at the University of Greenwich. First, through Greenwich Park, with its grand buildings

& open spaces. In this journey, as I had glimpsed Canary Wharf, so I had a quick view of the Millennium Dome, like a giant blancmange with wafers sticking out of it. In my infrequent visits, I still see London open-mouthed, as I did when I was a boy, on rare train journeys into Waterloo, as the river and the Houses of Parliament came into sight through spaces between buildings. In a way, it is still, for me, a city of romance, though now it is not only the storied old or new buildings – The Tower, St Paul's Cathedral, the Millennium Dome – that comprises the romance, but also the many different peoples, and mosques and Hindu temples as well as Wren churches. I *feel* the truth of Joe's statement that everyone should have the experience of living in London. I feel it in my own case anyway, although I also know that it is too late now – too late for the year or two I should have spent in London, before returning to live in the country.

In a room in the Riverside Building I was introduced to Sarah Smith, whose thesis on Sidney Keyes I had examined. Here, with Caroline, another colleague of John's, we held the *viva*, which was a fairly informal discussion of Keyes's life and work. Afterwards, when we had congratulated Sarah and before we had lunch, she showed me some items from the Keyes archive. A Keyes family photograph album – poignant for its own sake, but also because one family album is in some ways much like another, so that in this one I also saw images of my own childhood and my brothers' – at the seaside, in a pram, in the garden, with older relatives, a smiling curly headed boy or girl, just like Tony. Handwritten poems by Keyes – clear writing, passages scribbled over and revised, the brown spots of age on the paper, like the spots on an old person's hands.

My father was very original. He didn't look English; his handsome, sensitive face wasn't like any other English face I had ever seen. But what is 'English'? One of Dad's grandmothers was Irish. I was in my forties before I learnt that his father, Thomas Alfred, who was illegitimate, had had a Welsh father.

Mother told me the story. She had known Miss Hooker when she was an old lady, and found her frightening; a tall, silent old woman dressed all in black, who moved with much creaking of whalebone corsets, and who had been a Victorian lady's maid. Miss Hooker was the image of propriety, even the symbol of official Victorian morality, but evidently she had 'slipped' once, when she met a military bandsman, a Welshman called Evans, on board a liner on a sea voyage.

Their son, Tom Hooker, was brought up by his uncle, and went to work as a boy in the gardens of an estate. I have a photograph over my desk of the estate's workforce, of which he is the youngest, a boy (in whose face one can see Tony's) standing beside his massively bearded uncle, who is leaning over the back of a donkey, surrounded by workmen and women, each with the tool of his or her occupation – spade, fork, scythe, pail, and so on. Later, during the period of Winston Churchill's boyhood, Tom became keeper of the orchids at Blenheim. It was here that he met the woman who became his wife, Annie Wastie who was, I believe, a maid in a house at Woodstock. My father, who was a romantic, described their marriage as 'a love match'. 'Make no mistake about that,' he said.

Dad was also, at times, inclined to upgrade his father, calling him 'Keeper of Orchids to the Duke of Marlborough'. This, no doubt, was meant to counteract my equally romantic, inverted snobbery. But I was, I think, more in the right of it: Tom Hooker was a gardener, and a very good one. He was a little, wiry man with a great mass of white hair. I remember him in his 80s and 90s, when we would occasionally go to county cricket matches together, and it was unclear who was looking after whom. He had been a good cricketer, and was said to have played, at least once, in a team captained by Lord Tennyson. He and my father had both played for Sarisbury Green. Tom was a habitual smoker, whose longevity helped to justify my habit for the twenty years that it lasted; he used to buy the cheapest brand of cigarettes, which were called Turf and were the last to have a card, albeit unsatisfactorily attached to the inner cardboard of the packet; these he would break up, stuffing the tobacco in his pipe.

It would suit my self-image to be able to say that Tom Hooker, like the forebears Raymond Williams writes about in *The Country and the City*, had an acute sense of social injustice, and was preoccupied by wages and the class struggle. But the truth is Tom loved an aristocrat, or, to be more accurate, the owner of a big house. Wherever he went with my parents, when they took him for drives in the car in Hampshire, he would know the names of the people in the manor houses, and, to my mother's silent fury, would always expatiate on the charm of his lordship and her ladyship. He was also on friendly terms with many of the gardeners and house servants. Mother did once lose her temper with him, telling him the 'real lady' was in the kitchen, where Annie was preparing the supper.

It would be an understatement to say that Dad didn't get on with his father. Late in his own life, he mellowed somewhat towards him. But he always felt that his father had treated him harshly. The reason for this was that Aubrey was artistic. Not only did he have a fine singing voice, but, from the age of six, he showed a real talent for painting and drawing, including a wonderful sense of colour. His mother encouraged him, buying him his first paintbox. But Tom thought anything artistic a complete waste of time, and insisted that Aubrey leave school at the age of eleven and follow him into gardening, to supplement the family's modest income.

Now I think again about the subject, I can see that Dad's resentment towards his father must have influenced his relationship with his own first-born son (Dad was the eldest of four boys). A further sad irony is that Dave, sick to the back teeth (he would have said) with his father's talk about art and music, reacted strongly against 'culture', and decided to have absolutely nothing to do with it. He deliberately turned in the opposite direction, towards everything that was mechanical and practical (but with some incompetence in the latter respect that infuriated Dad). Only when he was about sixty did he discover the pleasure of reading the classics, and then he read all of Dickens's novels, followed by Tolstoy's. Poetry meant nothing to him. Mother noticed, however, that when Dad sang the old songs, Dave left the room to conceal the tears in his eyes. He was like his father in being sentimental, but I never heard the word 'culture' spoken with such scorn as when he used it.

Dad was artistic, but he wasn't educated. He had a deep emotional intelligence, but he wasn't intellectual. This showed in his art, for he loved the paintings of Constable above all, and then the work of the Impressionists, Pissarro, Monet, and Sisley. To him, Picasso and the whole of modern art were 'stunts'. In subject and execution his own landscape paintings were traditional, but they were not second-hand. He was a self-proclaimed 'perfectionist', who destroyed far more paintings than he allowed to survive. The handful still in existence show a vivid and subtle sense of colour and rhythmic movement; in fact, they realize an original perception of nature, of being in the natural continuum of sky and shadow, trees and water. They constitute a vision of peace, ego-less, free of all nervous agitation, and untouched by the modern world.

I didn't really look at my father's paintings when I was a boy. By the time that I did look at them, in my twenties, I was aware of our differences. One of these was symbolized by our attitudes towards a distinctive feature of the landscape, Sway Tower. Also known as Peterson's Tower, this is a major landmark of the southern New Forest and coastal area, and to me, because of the part it has played in my life, a sacred object. Rising to over two hundred feet out of a fairly flat landscape, the tower was built in the

1880s, by Andrew Thomas Turton Peterson, a retired Judge of the High Court of Calcutta. Peterson evidently combined mysticism and practical inventiveness, and was a man with radical sympathies. His aims in building the tower were to prove the strength and durability of reinforced concrete and to provide local unemployed men with work. True perhaps to its oriental and mystical inspiration, there is something preternatural about Sway Tower. Glimpsed from a corner of the eye, it can appear like a cobra enchanted by a fakir's pipe, or a phallus. Peterson probably intended the peculiarity. He was a spiritualist, and he believed that he had received architectural directions from Sir Christopher Wren through a medium. Peterson intended to have his ashes contained in an urn and placed at the summit of the tower, but was frustrated in that desire, and they were, I believe, interred at its base. Peterson understood, perhaps, the magical effect of landmarks upon those who live their lives in sight of them, so that they become woven into living experience, and thus perpetuate the memory of their builders by making it, for other people, subconsciously, part of the very ground of their being.

As I came to appreciate my father's paintings, and to see the rivers and fields of my home area anew through them, I thought how wonderful it would be if he were to paint a landscape containing Sway Tower, which can be seen from West Wight and the Solent, as well as from many parts of the New Forest. But, when I mentioned this wish to him, Dad curtly dismissed the tower as 'that eyesore, it should never have been built'. I was aware by that time of how much my way of seeing things, in my poetry, owed to his painterly vision of landscapes and places. So the dismissive remark gave me quite a shock, like the jarring blow on a 'funny' bone. Of course, I should have known. Did I really expect (it was another of my thoughts at the time) that he would paint a seascape containing an Esso tanker?

Aubrey had spent his early years in the north of England, and retained a Yorkshire accent lifelong. He came south in what he called 'a green winter'. The words expressed his air of slight condescension towards the south and southerners. He wasn't really of a tougher breed – quite the contrary – but he had known hard conditions, and he liked people to know that he came from a world that was more real than the soft south. He was 25 when he met my mother, who was 19. She first heard and saw him singing and playing the piano at a musical evening at a house in Sarisbury Green. She always remembered the comment an old man made at their wedding: 'Why, you're just two children'.

It was a love match, no doubt of that. My parents were married to each other for 60 years, and they were always romantic lovers. As far as I am able to judge, this was the most important factor in the shaping of my character. For good and ill. It could be said, of course, that it reflected my way of seeing things. I would say that I see things as I do because of their influence. What their feelings for each other gave me was the sense that love is the strongest force in human experience. It is this not only because it binds people to one another but because it colours their entire relationship to the world. To this sense I owe, also, an exaggerated idealism, which led me, too early, to want to replicate my parents' marriage, as I perceived it. I was thus self-blinded to the many human motives that have no tincture of love.

My father was the romantic. My mother, I came to realise, was the more loving one, unselfish, accepting, intensely loyal. I will not be able to portray her well. In choosing to write his *Autobiography* without reference to women, John Cowper Powys made things easier for himself. It is usually assumed that this ploy enabled him to avoid the hurt to others, especially the wife from whom he was estranged, that would have resulted from his treatment of love-affairs. As I contemplate writing about my mother it strikes me that the most likely reason for Powys's decision would have been in order to avoid having to write about *his* mother, to whom he was close, and whom he could not have mythologized as he did his father. Whether one is conscious of it or not, a mother is usually too close for myth: flesh of one's flesh. Speaking of her father, my mother once said: 'he's part of us, we're part of him'. How write *about* a person who is part of oneself? In the writing itself there will be an implicit revelation of that other person; but it will be impossible to find the distance necessary to *see* her.

In this connection I should say that I believe we reveal ourselves most truly not through self-analysis, but when we are looking away from ourselves, describing how we see and feel about someone or something else. It follows from this that I would regard any such self-revelation on my mother's part infinitely more valuable than anything I could say about her. Apart from family letters, she left very little of a personal nature. Indeed, after her death, I found, in the small notebook in which she copied out quotations, only one piece of her own writing. It is called 'A Country Walk 1917'.

It is spring and the sky is blue and the lane is deeply rutted
by carts so we walk on the grass verge and explore the ditch

and bank. The ditch is partly filled with clear running water and look, near the bottom in a patch of sunshine there is a clump of lesser celandines. I remember the poem recently learnt, "There is a flower, the lesser celandine that shrinks, like many more from cold and rain, bright as the sun it is out again". And do look there is the first primrose, "A primrose awoke from its long winter sleep and stretched out its head through its green leaves to peep".

Later on we came back primrosing and carried armfuls of the delicate flowers, but that was a pleasure to come.

We stand and gaze in wonder at a clump of wild violets but do not pick them as their stems are too fragile and the little heads will soon droop "All things bright and beautiful, the Lord God made them all".

We stride the ditch and peep over the bank to see a white field of wood anemones, lovely flower fairies, and among them the green shoots of bluebells.

We reach to touch the tails of hazel catkins and powder our hand with the yellow pollen.

Now we reach the gate but although it is open we climb the stile and know that the stinging nettles will sting our legs, but there is always a dock leaf near and we rub our legs until the green juice stains them.

My friends swing on the gate but I sit on the stile and look up in wonder at the blue sky and the fleecy clouds. "The clouds were pure and white as flocks new shorn, sweetly they slept on the blue fields of Heaven". Heaven, that is where my mother is but I hug a secret to myself. Every night when my candle is out my mother comes to me as a shining light in the corner of my bedroom.

Now we walk back to the conker tree, grown ups call it sycamore and someone once hid in a sycamore tree to see

Jesus but I forget his name. The buds are so delightfully sticky but will soon burst into leaf and later in the year the boys will collect the conkers and tie them onto pieces of string for their annual game.

Prince, the farm horse is coming down the lane so it must be nearly tea time as he always knows when there is a knob of sugar for him. Patient Prince with his enormous white body and feathered feet. The farm cat has all her kittens in his manger and knows he would rather go hungry than harm them. Another manger once held something that was bigger than all the world and yet can live in the seed of the smallest flower.

We return home as the sun is going down and there is a patch of sunlight still in the wood which fills us with pleasure but we do not know why this is. Grandfather used to say, 'patches of Godlight'.

Some part of my father's attraction to my mother was played by her education. At 25, he could barely write; he had no book knowledge, and only a rudimentary notion of 'manners'. From the beginning, he had a touching faith in her knowledge and refinement. She had been clever and artistic in school, and she had become a primary school teacher; when they met, she had a job in the Ministry of Employment in Southampton. As I have said, my mother heard him singing, in the house of a mutual acquaintance, before they were introduced. They went out walking together. He joked about it in later years: she was wearing a particular perfume: 'I was a lost man'. Of course, he meant *found*.

The young Ivy Mould was very attractive; she was also gentle and kind, with a genuine innocence, which would be very difficult for later generations to understand. She knew and loved poetry, which she could quote, from her school book, *Laureata*, which, like Palgrave's *Golden Treasury*, was an anthology rich in the English lyrical tradition. For Aubrey, this was part of her wonderful educated intelligence. Soon they were engaged and taking excursions together; at that time he had a motorbike; once, coming off the Woolston floating-bridge, he travelled some distance before realising that he hadn't given her time to get on the pillion. One day, picnicking on Butser Hill, a wasp got down the back of her gauzy blouse – to the consternation of both, since he couldn't possibly remove it from there. She gave up her career for him. That, of course, was the story of many women of my mother's generation. It never occurred to her that there was an alternative, and all the evidence suggests she never wished there was. This was more believable in that she never lost her own voice. She would not confront him over some issues in which he should not have been able to get his own way. She was afraid of his temper, his verbal violence, and the bad nerves with which he would periodically torment himself, and make life difficult for her. But she retained her independence of mind, and her interest in people and nature and books. In old age, she talked to me about herself, as she had never spoken to anyone before. I learnt then that she had a strong sense of inner self, an inviolable and incommunicable inner 'place' or core. My father was probably too romantic about himself to be capable of much self-analysis. My mother knew both him and herself extremely well.

She had a strong will, which could make her rigidly unjust in defence of those she loved. I grew up with a very harsh view of her stepmother, Aunty May, an old woman with little to commend her to a small boy. She was mousy and very pious, living her life by the tenets of the Gospel Hall; an archetypal follower of 'creeping Jesus', I would have said then, and if no one encouraged me in this, no one would have corrected me, either. Ivy's mother had died in child birth in 1917, leaving Pop with four daughters and one son to bring up. The story I received from my mother was that, before his marriage, he had known May's sister, who was generous and life-loving, and, the sister now being married, had made the mistake of thinking May would be like her. But Ivy had loved her mother; as she described in her essay, she felt her mother's presence in the corner of her bedroom after her death; it is unlikely that any woman could have taken her place in Ivy's affections.

May certainly could not. According to Mother, when Pop lay dying, he told her that May was praying him to death. Another story was of May rebuking Pop for going to the pictures. How would he feel if Jesus returned to earth and found him in such a place? Pop replied that he could imagine much worse places in which he might be found.

Whatever the story, the laugh was always on Aunty May. Consequently I felt deeply ashamed when, sometime after Mother's death, Tony casually remarked that May was a brave woman. Startled, I asked him what he meant. He then pointed out what should have been obvious to me: that she had 'taken on' a man with five children and a dubious reputation as far as women were concerned. In more than fifty years, it had never occurred to me that there might be any discrepancy between Mother's version of things and the truth. I don't say now that the latter is the exact truth, any more than the former; only that I should have considered the possibility of another version than that which I had received.

It is all too easy in writing about the past to convey an external impression of events, so that even to oneself people one has loved and known become actors with names, characters in a story. Obviously, every autobiographical sketch is a form of fiction. We are all inveterate storytellers to ourselves and others about our own lives, and we come to know ourselves in and by the stories we tell. Photographs are at least as bad as fiction in this respect. Sometimes, however, a photograph may suggest the possibility of a different kind of knowledge. Thus, in thinking about Pop and Aunty May, I am now remembering one photograph in particular. Actually, it is a sequence of amateur snaps of one scene: a family group, now with one or several members out of the picture, taken at different angles outside a tin shed situated between Canterbury House and Southampton Cooperative Society. In one snap, the LD of MOULD can be seen below part of the window of Pop's junk shop. And there, in the snaps, are the older couple, Pop and May, and my brothers, young men standing at the back, and my father, and Mother's eldest (and favourite) sister, Aunty Kitty, and Uncle Tom, and their two sons. In two of the snaps I am standing in front of Mother, who is holding me, gently but firmly, with her hands on my shoulders. She is a young woman, I am perhaps four years old. There is nothing in the least remarkable about this family group, which could be roughly dated by the clothes and by the look of the Co-op. But for me, as I look at the sulky, discontented expression on my face, and at my legs in short trousers, I can *feel* my legs pressing back against Mother, and my body wriggling to escape her hold, and the muscles in the face I am pulling, and I want there to be an end to this tedium, so that I can be away from there, AWAY, running, stretching my limbs in freedom.

20 November

Dad's birthday today; he would have been 98, a year older than his father when *he* died.

I see in the local newspaper that the young woman who for a time occupied the hospital bed opposite me, has died.

On a cold, bright morning I walked alone to the post office to buy stamps and post letters. This excursion, which involves crossing the road at the traffic lights, would have been beyond me even quite recently.

Now, on a quiet Saturday morning, I sit at my desk. There are fewer leaves on the birch, almost all of them yellow, and they create that extra light, shining into my window, which is so beautiful on fine days at this time of year. They are moving gently in an easterly breeze, and I feel that I should be able to see the Westbury White Horse, on the hill several miles away, in a space between the leaves; but although I have seen it on several occasions when a leaf has moved, I can't see it today.

In the land which I can see, hedged and lightly wooded green fields, with a few farm buildings, between the near roofs of Frome and the downs above Warminster, runs the boundary between Somerset and Wiltshire. When I came back to England eleven years ago and lodged initially with Les and Sandy at their farm at Bradford on Avon, I hoped that Mieke and I would find a permanent home in Wiltshire. Instead, we bought a house in Somerset, but with a study window through which I can look into the other county.

To me, Wiltshire has always been ancestral ground. Mother's people on her mother's side, the Elkins, came from Bishopstone, a village near Salisbury, and her uncle was bailiff on the Wilton estate, to which he could walk from his home. Mother's parents were married at the church at Bishopstone, and were so poor that the vicar would not take their marriage fee. In old age, Mother sent a contribution, with an explanatory letter, to the present incumbent.

Her stories of her relatives, who worked on the land, inspired my feelings for Wiltshire. But the feelings were given a body, as it were, by my childhood visits to the Devenings, and my fascination with the White Horse, and Silbury Hill, and the barrows. More than this, it was a kind of falling in love with the landscape itself, with the oceanic swell of the open downs, and the formative rock, chalk laid bare in a cutting, whitish fields of chalk and flints. Like sexual love, this feeling for land has an integral physical component; it isn't only about looking – the lust of the eye – but about wanting to plant one's feet on the soil, and walk on the springy sward of the downs. Wordsworth spoke of the appetite he had as a boy for climbing mountains, and I know what he meant – appetite is the right word – although the landscapes I cleave to are less dramatic than his were.

There were other influences on my feelings for Wiltshire, too. When we moved to Hayford I became friends with a boy who lived in a bungalow across the way from me, in Northover Road. His name was Charlie Dance, and he had a free and open nature. Already at 8 years of age, Charlie knew not only what he wanted to do but to *be*: a farmer. He had an uncle who owned a farm in Wiltshire, and one day he took me there with him on a visit. I wish I could remember where it was and the actual details of the place. All that I can call to mind is a sense of quintessential *Wiltshire farm*: a barn raised on concrete 'mushrooms', swallows flying in and out of the barn and round the stone farmhouse, cows and dungy smells, pasture and ploughland sloping up from the buildings, which were grouped together in a scoop of the land. And that is all, but what I remember is a wonderful sense of freedom, the freedom to play in the barn and yard and among the hedges and fields, and a feeling of belonging, which I caught from Charlie.

Years later, when I did some research into conditions in rural Southern England at the time of the Swing riots, in 1830, I came upon a reference to a James Mould, a young labourer with a large family, who had been transported from Wiltshire to Van Diemen's Land for his part in the agitations. By then, I was no longer living in the south of England, though to do so was the thing I wanted more than anything else. On journeys home, the whitening of fields and the smooth sweep of chalk hills, in Wiltshire, filled me with nostalgic longing. But by then, too, I recognised the emptiness of the land. It was literally the space without people, since far fewer were needed to run the agricultural industry, than farming had required in the past. It was also the partial evacuation of my own romanticism, since I now knew something about what it meant to be bound to the soil, or torn from it, as James Mould had been, which I hadn't known when Charlie and I had played together on his uncle's farm. Yet it is quite possible that Charlie had found what he had wanted. I hope he did. I knew, however, that whatever 'belonging' I might achieve, it wasn't on the land in Wiltshire; though the knowledge didn't stop me wanting.

Still, the view from my study window, through the leaves or bare branches of the birch-tree, towards Warminster and Cley Hill and the country towards Salisbury beyond, means more to me than I can say. I had seen the same inarticulacy in my mother. Early one August, on her birthday, I had taken her in the car on a journey in quest of the place where Pop was born. This was in the region of Martin, on the Wiltshire-Hampshire border, where W.H. Hudson had gathered the materials for his *A Shepherd's Life*. We knew the name of the place as Allen Toyd, but although we found the river Allen and Toyd Down, we did not find Pop's birthplace. What I saw in my mother's face as we drove about that country on our quest was the feeling which she had, she said, 'in my blood'. I could no more describe the feeling than she could, and while alerted by my intellect to distance myself from any notions of 'blood and soil', I felt that it had to do with the sensation of particular earth underfoot, and one's physical relation to the rhythms of the landscape, and to knowledge, in this place, of the livingness of those now dead, to whom one owed one's own life.

Later Towards dusk, though only 3.45 pm, sky overcast. All the little leaves on the birch are moving in what must be a cold wind – a shivering movement, which is also like a flickering of small yellow flames.

Once started on my autobiographical sketches I find it difficult to stop; but I have to, in order to turn my attention, for part of the time, to work on my critical book, 'Imagining Wales'. So this afternoon I have been going over my notes on John Cowper Powys, especially on *Owen Glendower* and *Porius* – again, enough notes to provide the materials for a book, though I am only going to write one chapter.

The temerity with which I first wrote on Powys, 25 years ago, on the basis of one incomplete reading, now seems to me astonishing. Evidently I wasn't then obsessed by the search for a key to all mythologies. In fact, I wrote with excitement, and perhaps with more self-trust – or less scholarly caution – than I later granted myself.

In the years between, as I have reread JCP, my wonder has grown, though at times his wordiness still infuriates me. Or disappoints, when it marks a failure of the poetic spirit. Nor am I entirely reconciled to his 'escapism', even if I understand it better now. But the fundamental cause of my excitement and wonder remains – the sense of possibility which results from his sceptical treatment of all knowledge (philosophy, science, and psychology, as well as mere knowingness) and reverence for nature. The latter includes his faith in the power of the human mind, with its faculties of will and imagination, to create the world in which each being lives. Indeed, he extends the power beyond humans to other creatures. It is a *faith*, or it is based on his own life-illusion as a magician. It is terribly vulnerable to all the proponents of scientific materialism and psychology. But their dogmas are vulnerable in turn to Powys's idea of imagination. And in this I find his thought and story-telling exhilarating, as it wrecks the dogmas that cage our minds – Marxism, scientism, Freudian & Jungian psychology – and liberates us to remake ourselves by telling other stories.

21 November

While Mieke stayed in bed with 'flu symptoms, I walked alone down Culver Hill and up to Spar to buy a newspaper this morning, the first time since the stroke that I have made this excursion on my own. A bright, shining morning, cloudless overhead, though Cley Hill & the Longleat woods were lightly veiled in mist. The small tortoiseshell cat was sitting right on top of its bungalow roof, full in the sun, pretending not to be watching a party of pigeons on the dew-wet grass below. A friendly sight to me, as many things are in the immediate surroundings, which I wouldn't have noticed once. Late flowers, for example, in bungalow gardens, bright yellow & blue pansies against moist, brown soil. Now they remind me of my first outing into the hospital gardens, taking a few steps round flower-beds, with a nurse pushing a wheelchair behind me – the look of the growing flowers, the smell of the earth.

Walking back with the sun behind me, my long shadow went in front, reminding me that I was walking with sticks. At times now I forget, although I am reminded also by the sight of older men or women walking normally, when I become mindful of my own clumsier, slower progress.

The primary school I attended for one year was at Lock's Heath, near Warsash, and not far from Canterbury House and Camiola, the house in which my father's parents lived. I recall little about the school except the different pleasurable sensations of raffia and plasticine on my fingers and in my nose, and the majestic bigness of the older boys and girls, which I couldn't imagine attaining. I felt the same as little Thomas Traherne did, in seventeenth-century Hereford, only it was eight-year old boys and girls, not aged men, who seemed to me 'venerable and reverend creatures'.

At that time the attitude towards me of older children, especially girls, was nurturing. It was a grown-up girl, as I thought of her, who showed me how to look at the line of a house roof against the sky, on the opposite side of Greenaway Lane, so that I saw, with a sudden giddy sensation, the rapid movement of the turning Earth. I always knew where to look for the movement after that, and was never again deceived by the notion that things stand still.

The third school I attended in three years, after Miss Wemys's was in Southampton. The name and address are imprinted on my mind, as some are when one remembers little of the place itself: St Nicholas, Bassett Crescent West. The journey to and from school made a deeper impression on me: bus or car from Warsash to Woolston, across the Itchen on the floating-bridge, tram through Southampton city centre and up the Avenue, leaving a short walk to St Nicholas. From these journeys, the floating-bridge became very dear to me. It was a ferry on chains, which went down mysteriously into milky green water, with drawbridges at either end, to let vehicles and foot passengers off and on. Eventually it was made redundant by the new Itchen Bridge, and was converted into a night club, and finally destroyed by fire. But to anyone who had known it, and especially as a child, the floating-bridge had been a thing of myth, which afforded a crossing between worlds.

On the journeys, I was in the charge of an older boy who lived in a bigger house further up Greenaway Lane. He was a friend, or at least, not an enemy, when we were on home ground and under the eyes of our respective parents, and I liked to play with him and his younger brother, because their father had made them an almost full-sized model Spitfire, in which we could take turns sitting at the controls, each imagining himself one of the few. Once at school, however, my protector became a bully, and a leader of bullies, one of whose amusements was to cage me under a desk in the classroom at break, and hit my legs with rulers.

If I didn't complain at this treatment – and I don't recall that I did - the reason was that, by the age of six, I had started to pride myself on being stoical. This took the form of not showing hurt of any kind. On one occasion, for example, I was walking across the football pitch at St Nicholas's when an older boy, shooting at goal with all his might, hit me full in the face with the football, which knocked me flat on my back. Dazed and smarting fearfully from the blow, I got up and walked away, with the older boys' commendations of my bravery ringing in my ears.

I strove to turn the same face to emotional hurt. Two years after this incident, when I was at school at Rope Hill, the question of 'character' arose in class. We had a new teacher, a young man called Mr Valentine who had red hair. My class mates (I was a quiet boy at that time) sought his opinion of Andrew Jack, a good-natured troublemaker, one of twelve brothers whose father was a farmer at Saxmundham; like me, Jack (we called each other by our surnames at Rope Hill) had a local accent, which made him funnier.

'Jack,' said Mr Valentine, 'has great character.'

And what about Hooker? my classmates asked.

'Hooker,' said Mr Valentine, 'has no character at all.'

It wasn't meant as a joke, but, with a forced smile on my face, I pretended that it was, though if I could have ceased to exist at that moment, and for some time afterwards, I would eagerly have done so.

I have since wondered where this need to appear stoical came from. From my mother, I think, for it was in her nature; and from Tony, the King's scout who did not flinch at pain, or cry. And perhaps also as an instinctive reaction against my father, who was an emotional and highly nervous man.

The most amazing thing he ever said to me was when he was in the nursing home, near the end of his life:

'You're like me, Jerry, you're not afraid of anything.'

It would have been much nearer the truth if he had said the opposite.

He was afraid of thunderstorms, and showed his fear. He was afraid of heights, and communicated his fear to me through the pressure of his hand on mine, and his crouching posture near the wall, as we climbed some not very steep steps. He was afraid of open spaces, and took me as a companion on walks and drives, as a kind of protection against the terror of space. 'Terror' seems an exaggeration, but it was the only word that corresponded to my feelings when, as a young man, I suddenly began to suffer from agoraphobia.

I came to know my father's fear in my own nerves. Mother told me the story of how, once, when he was a young sales representative for a seeds firm, travelling alone by car in north Wiltshire, he had been forced to stop at a pub, not for a drink but to regain his sanity by exchanging a few words with another human being, and to phone his brother to come and get him and the car, because he was incapable of driving on. I knew the story as soon as I was told it, not as a verbal narrative, but as a tightening of all my limbs, a high singing note in my head, difficulty in breathing and swallowing, and the word *can't* like an insurmountable obstacle in my path. *I CAN'T GO ON.*

It has only occurred to me in later years that my father was a brave man. Once, at Hayford, a crash of thunder coincided with lightning striking a power cable near the house, and Dad literally ran round the room crying out, 'Who should we be helping?' He was as scared as I was, but he was ready to help – for him, it was the Blitz all over again. Due to his age, he had been too young to fight in the First World War and too old to serve in the Second. But in the latter he had been a billeting officer responsible for rehousing families bombed out of their homes in Portsmouth, and, unlike me, he had real terrible memories. I realised, too, that being so tormented by his nerves, it had been brave of him to go out at all, travelling to earn a living.

I may have reacted against my father's emotionalism when I was a boy; there is no doubt that I did so later. Unlike most other Englishmen I have met, my father told stories with the emotional stops out. Many of them were about himself, and some involved his father's lack of understanding of him, or slights that he had received over the years. Or they were about his mother, whom he loved and revered as a saintly woman, or about Ivy and her wonderful mind. He cried easily. But he also conveyed a terrific sense of his enjoyment of life. Regularly at Christmas, for example, after one small drink, he would dance around the roast turkey waving the carving knife, and singing loudly. I am ashamed to say that I was always apprehensive of him attending my lectures or poetry readings, in case, as not infrequently happened, he would start crying, audibly.

But whether my father was laughing or crying there was a period in my life, when I was a young man, when I couldn't bear him being emotional. Then, when he showed signs of beginning, I would make an excuse to leave the room, and walk to the end of the garden, where I would stand still, breathing deeply. Or, if I stayed in the room, the more he let himself go, the more the muscles of my face tautened, as though my flesh were turning to wood, and I looked on like a carved mask. It seemed to me at such times that, with his deep sense of self, and of the drama of his own existence, he took up all the emotional space, and left no room for others.

'Deep', in fact, was one of my father's favourite words, and although it seemed to me in those days that he mediated everything through his own experience, I knew that he was a deep man, a man whose feeling for nature and for human experience and relationships between men and women was profound, and made him an original thinker. I never actually wished that another man was my father, but I did sometimes wish my father was another man.

A friend who read my first collection of essays in typescript told me that I overused the word 'deep'. I saw that he was right, and, for myself, I saw my overfondness for superlatives – it was as though, in writing about people and things, I was incapable of irony, and inclined naturally to celebration.

At the present, I have not been able to decide upon a memorial for my parents. There is nothing to mark Pop's grave in the churchyard at Sarisbury Green. He had made it understood that he didn't want anything

– 'if people cared to remember me,' he said, 'they would'. Mother took the same view as far as she herself was concerned.

I had found it easy to decide about the disposal of her ashes, since she loved the sea, and especially the sea within view of the Isle of Wight, which she had lived in sight of for much of her life. In her last years, we had frequently gone together to the cliffs or beach at Barton on Sea, so that when we scattered her ashes there, on a beautiful and serene All Souls Day, it had felt right.

My father was another matter. I knew, from very occasional remarks, that he would have expected a 'good' funeral, with music and many mourners and an emotional atmosphere. But, in the event, he outlived most of his contemporaries, and all but a few of those who survived were too old or too ill to attend. So the service preceding his cremation was a small, fairly utilitarian affair, which would have been partially redeemed for him by the attendance of two old men, growers he had helped during his days as an advisory officer in the New Forest, who had read of his death and the time of the service in a newspaper. Afterwards I drove round for some months with his ashes in an urn in the boot of the car.

He wouldn't have wanted them scattered on the sea, because he didn't like the sea. He always said it was 'too turbulent', and insisted that he loved nature in a peaceful mood. He needed peace as well, to counter the inner turbulence which frightened him. In consequence, his paintings were mainly of rivers: places of light and shadow, movement and stillness, where force is channelled, and contained. I had a range of choice for the disposal of his ashes – somewhere on the Hampshire Avon, say, or the Stour, or the Wylye, or the Lymington River. But still I prevaricated.

Why? I think the reason was my sense of the diminution he would have felt. Both my parents had been great powers in my life. The memorial service which we were able to hold for my mother – before death or debility had taken so many of my parents' friends – and also the magnificence of the sea, seemed to match her spirit. But to scatter all that remained of my father on a river?

I felt the guiltier at seeing the joke in this hesitation, which left the ashes in the car boot. And at last I decided, with Mieke, to scatter them on a secluded stretch of the Lymington River, between Boldre Bridge and Boldre Church, both of which he had made oil paintings. So it was done, on a day in early spring, when the pale yellow of primroses and bright yellow of first daffodils showed among the oak trees – those near the river with flood-mark tufts of grass caught in their lower branches- on the bank.

Even so, I felt the place meant more to me than it would have done to him – there was so much of his life that it excluded.

These events were shadowed by the general problem of the lack of an adequate ritual for those who no longer live – or die - within a community and a communal belief. The funeral director with whom I had made arrangements for my father's cremation had told me a touching story. In his storeroom he had an urn of ashes which had remained uncollected for several years. First a gipsy had died and been cremated, and his wife had asked the funeral director to hold onto the urn until after her death and cremation, when her ashes would be mixed with her husband's, and their son would collect the urn. In due course the woman died, and her wishes were honoured. Then the son appeared at the funeral parlour, but, instead of claiming the urn, he requested that, when he died and was cremated, his ashes would be mixed with his parents'. And who, I wondered, would collect the urn then? Clearly, with people as fiercely attached to their families as gypsies, the process could be repeated for as long as one family member remained alive. And then what would become of the urn?

It was a good story; but it didn't help me to decide upon a memorial for my parents. Was I wrong not to have buried their ashes together under one stone? Possibly. But where? At Sarisbury Green, outside the church in which they had been married, but where they hadn't been for many years? In the churchyard at Pennington, where they had attended services while living at Hayford (but where Dad, while he could still see, looked with horror at the uniform white grave stones)? Or at Old Milton, where they spent their last years together?

In the end, I had given their ashes to the separate elements they loved, and had postponed the decision on a joint memorial. And the underlying reason for this, I realized, was that they were identified for me, not with one place, but with the whole of that country – the Wiltshire Downs, where my mother's people had come from, the New Forest, especially the area between the southern Forest and the Isle of Wight, all the land that lies below you as, driving from Brockenhurst, you come over the ridge at Marlpit Oak. And there was another reason too, which diminished my feeling of guilt for failing to do what appeared to be the right thing: that they are alive for me, as presences, and in me, so that there is no one place which, while I live, I could think of as being their last.

22 November

Emily, slender and attractive, and Jason called in yesterday morning and I went with them to the Horse and Groom at East Woodlands for Sunday lunch.

Emily has switched from Business Studies to a Psychology course, and is finding it difficult, because she joined late and because of the demands of her other work on her time and energy. I am proud that my daughter is making her living by driving a delivery van, or lorry, her territory covering the area where my father once had his office, in Petersfield, *and* studying part-time.

It is deeply gratifying to me – and I'm sure to Emily, too – that we are close to each other again. We were very close when she was a little girl; later, with the marriage break-up and my move from the family home, distance inevitably grew between us. But what made it worse was my emotional need for her, and the pressure I unconsciously put on her when we were together. It is a fatal mistake to *ask* a child for love.

Sex is the ugliest word in the English language. I sometimes fancy that it might have been invented by the executive of an oil company, by analogy with the company's name and to designate the energy that drives life, fuelling and exhausting its individual vehicles, and with the sole purpose of keeping the traffic moving.

Its uses can be terrible: commodified, and in the mixing of hatred and contempt with desire in sexual relationships; its effects can be magical. Sex is not confined to the human sphere, of course, but is diffused through all our connections to the world, and through every strand in the web of nature. I cannot remember a time when I was not drawn to the female, or conceive of a world which is not pervaded by the aura of woman.

I was four or five when I first consciously made a fool of myself. Mother had taken me to see a show at the village hall at Sarisbury Green. We sat in the front row watching little girls dancing and singing, and one of them, with long fair hair and, like the others, wearing tights, enchanted me. There was no other word for it. I sat watching her alone, utterly besotted. And as I watched the desire to touch her became overwhelming. I knew this was forbidden, yet I contrived it. When the girls left the stage, I pretended to be asleep, with eyes closed, and as she passed in front of me, I fell off my chair and briefly clasped her, as one would do who was genuinely asleep and lost his balance. Mother, at least, was wise to the ruse, and afterwards observed, gently, that I had disgraced myself.

Living at Hayford, the first school I attended, also for a year, was Rowan College, one of the numerous, rather humble preparatory schools which, in those days, occupied the former houses of minor gentry in the south of England. Two events stand out from my recollections of this year. The first was falling in love – consciously, actually saying to myself, 'I am in love'. Karen Read wore her hair done up in two bobs at the back of her head, and was freckled and snub-nosed. So memory pictures her, but deceptively, for it completely omits the attraction that drew me, and pervaded her whole being. The closest I came to her was when I picked up her eraser from where it had fallen on the floor and returned it to her, winning a smile of gratitude. For mine was a hopeless love; she walked to and from school hand in hand with David Rice, a sportsman and wit who, at 8 years of age, was as glamorous to my envious eyes as a matinee idol.

I recall no lessons from Rowan College, though I was roused by some of the hymns we sang, such as 'Eternal Father, strong to save', 'We plough the fields and scatter', and Isaac Watts' (as I would learn) 'Our God, our help'. The other memorable occasion was a stroll, arm in arm, with my friend Brian Morgan, a Welsh boy from Monmouth, who lived in Pennington for a year or two. As we were walking along, affectionately, in the school grounds, a group of boys suddenly appeared coming towards us, my friend Roger Doman among them. Immediately I disentangled my arm from Brian's and pretended to be fighting him. An unsuccessful ruse, which the other boys saw through at once, and started taunting us. In Roger's contemptuous eyes, I glimpsed also a look of sadness and reproach.

It is easy enough to indulge oneself with recollections, amusing or charming oneself, or inflating minor accidents or misfortunes into horrors. I am not immune to the temptation. What interests me much more, though, is the sensation of life, and how, through experience, one grows into the world, simultaneously forming a mind and imagination – a personality – and connections to people and things and places. Thus, as I lay in hospital, it was moments that returned to me. Not simply events I could partially envisage, but the sensation of being: a moment in the midst of life, my life, which no one else could ever know, and which, for me, had an intimacy I could not describe. This once-and-for-ever-unrepeatable sensation is unique, yet also the commonest human experience. Perhaps that is why we rarely talk about it – the uniqueness makes dwelling on it seem an indulgence, the commonness inclines us to take it for granted. And in consequence something vital is missing from our knowledge of ourselves and of each other, and an impenetrable mystery surrounds all human experience.

'We live – as we dream – alone', says Marlow in *Heart of Darkness*. Yes; but we enter into one another's dreams, too, and our dream-worlds share landscapes and stories. As a child, I sometimes knew when I was dreaming, and then I knew that I could enjoy myself with impunity, flying, for example, without fear of falling. The strength of my feeling for Tony was certainly increased by the dream occasion when, walking through the gravel cut at Priestlands, between Lymington and Pennington, a small blue butterfly landed on one of my fingers, and gripped it, like a tight-fitting ring, and would not let go. I was terrified and my hand was hurting, when my brother appeared, as he had when I was wandering in the dangerous wood, and pulled the butterfly off.

On that occasion, I did not know that I was dreaming, but on another, conscious that I was, I held a sixpence in my hand and tried hard to do something that I longed to do: *bring something back*. Willing myself to wake up, I rose through layer after layer of sleep, like a diver coming up from deep water, keeping firm hold of the coin. It was still in my hand as I broke the surface, when a loud voice boomed in my ear, NO YOU DON'T, and I let the sixpence go. As I lay in my bed in the dark the room vibrated and echoed with the terrible voice, like a roll of thunder. Later, I would wonder what would have happened if I had held on, waking with the coin in my hand. I felt I would have died.

In hospital, I knew that what I wanted to record was happiness. The support of family and friends made me more than usually aware of how lucky I was, and, looking back, I felt that I had had an especially happy childhood, which I would like to leave a record of. But writing autobiographically, I find, means more than making a record. It is a process of discovery also, in which, as I have said before, fictional story-telling plays a part. I am, then, pursuing something elusive – how it felt to be alive then, when, at any given moment, I was held within my entire existence, and simultaneously open to an ever-expanding world.

I have spoken of recording, but what was actually happening to me in hospital, more often than not, was that moments were rising from the past, like bubbles containing pictures. They would surface, as I had emerged from the dreams – sensations of life, and, as one might try to pick up a coloured stone from shallow water and find it attached to the whole sea-bed, so I found the momentary sensation embedded in my very being, as it had been and as it was.

23 November

Mieke continues very poorly, weak and sleeping most of the time. I called a taxi and took her to the Health Clinic yesterday afternoon, and Dr Ellis gave her a prescription for antibiotics. I have seen her in this condition before. It is almost as though she goes into hibernation for several days, while nature effects the cure, and then emerges strengthened and refreshed. But I don't take anything for granted.

Sandy came in in the middle of the day and had a cup of tea with me. I told her about my morning walks, and how, since my period of convalescence at home, I have got to know more of the immediate area, and have spoken with more neighbours, than in the previous nine years that we have lived here. And this intimate knowing of place corresponds to my early instinctual attachments, which have been more theoretical than actual in recent years.

Sandy said this is women's experience – thus contradicting what Sarah Briggs had said to me: that my sense of place, as a man, was completely different from a woman's. Sandy told me that Les had had very little contact with people in Bradford on Avon, but, as I could well understand, spent most of his time at the college or on college work. She, on the other hand, gained a lot of pleasure and support from meeting neighbours, and from intimate knowledge of the town. She felt that this was generally the case in relationships where the man had work that took him away from the home and the woman spent most of her time at home and in the locality.

The conversation made me think again about my own sense of place. When I was a boy my local attachments were largely unconscious. Once I had left the south of England and was living in Wales, in my mid-twenties, I began to see home ground, Hayford and the immediate surroundings, the New Forest and the coastal area from Southampton to Christchurch, with special intensity, and to develop what the Welsh call *hiraeth* – longing for my native places. With marriage and the birth of my children, the feeling intensified.

As many people do, no doubt, I found that my children restored my own childhood to me. Delighting in them, and playing with them and telling them stories as they grow, reactivates one's own play instinct and what is called, sloppily, one's inner child. In my case, holiday visits to Hayford and my early landscapes enabled me to explore them again, with my children. Not always to our mutual happiness, I have to say. On one occasion I took them for a walk through gorse bushes on Wainsford Common and dense vegetation beside the Avon Water, and set off upstream, in an area which is magical to me, but where they were soon boot-clogged with sticky clay and scratched by prickles, and grizzled from boredom and exhaustion. By and large, however, our visits and explorations were mutually enjoyable. At the same time Joe and Emily were growing into life in Wales, in a way that brought me closer to Welsh neighbours and to the area in which we lived.

I cannot remember a time when I did not have a sense of the past. At first, it was the very remote past, visible in the land. As I grew up, my awareness of history broadened and deepened. The mixture of external events with personal memory was already evident when, as a boy, I was telling war stories. From my teens, nostalgia was strong – a few of us getting drunk together, seventeen year olds obsessed by girls and jazz and politics, would tell each other stories about our past.

But it was probably in the later period, when I was a young father that I came to see the truth of the Romantics' idea of childhood, as though I had always known it. Then, my particular version of it emphasised the connection between child and place. Whenever I visited any place that was new to me, I would find myself trying to imagine it as a child growing up there would see it. What I was after was the truth of an intimacy which has rarely been put into words, though it has been source of a great deal of poetry and art, especially in Britain, but perhaps in any long-settled country also. I was aware, for instance, of the way in which a person's language-sense develops in relation to particular people and things, and that in consequence a binding relationship between words and person and place grows in the mind. In my own case, words associated with water – shore, estuary, river, stream, brook, shingle, seawall, mudbank, creek, and so on – retained sense impressions of the Hamble River, the Solent, and New Forest streams. And words brought with them, as my mind developed, historical resonances – *Mary Rose, HMS Hood, RMS Titanic*, whose loss bereaved whole streets in Southampton – which attached me ever more intimately to a historical seascape and landscape.

As a young man rediscovering childhood, through his own children, I partly recovered and partly invented a sense of place. My memory, therefore, is mediated through this later period, so that I cannot always know whether it is a moment of childhood I am describing, or that moment as the man, with his *hiraeth*, reconstructed it. But in any event, there is always of course some degree of recreation.

This subject has a bearing on dependency. Most modern people, it seems, like to think of themselves as independent, and I am no exception.

I too could make a reasonable boast, Sinatra-like, of having done things my way. Yet I would have to admit to being also, in some ways, intrinsically dependent.

This is implicit in my thinking about place, which emphasises relationship: the ties that bind me to others, the intimate connection between language and sensation, and the growth of imagination in relation to particular people and localities and things. I value 'unlearning', the process of rejecting received opinions and conventional ways of seeing in the act of thinking for oneself; but my sense of being in the world implies relationship – to family and friends, to shaping historical experience, to the poetic traditions in which I discovered my love of poetry. What moves me more than anything is the experience or idea of sharing. What I most dread is total isolation – and it is 'thought' of that, even more than the process of dying, which I fear about death. Indeed, it is thought that is impossible to think, but in sickness or with sick people, in hospital for example, one can feel it and see it – as life withdraws behind the face, retreating from those eager to arrest it, to call the sick person back, into the only world we know, which is the one we share.

My father loved to hear my mother recite poetry. He genuinely liked poetry, but he took more delight in my mother's gift, which was a token of her education. She had been at school during the First World War, and the book from which she learnt poems by heart, *Laureata*, contained an admixture of lyrical verse and stirring narrative poems. From when I was quite small, she would recite to me poems from this book, as well as from R.L. Stevenson's *A Child's Garden of Verse*, which was the first poetry book I owned, together with nursery rhymes. There was also the small, blue-covered edition of the lyrics from Tennyson's *The Brook*, with Victorian pastoral vignettes, and this was the book from which I most liked to be read:

> I come from haunts of coot and hern,
>   I make a sudden sally,
> And sparkle out among the fern,
>   To bicker down a valley.

I responded with a pleasurable sadness to the idea of men coming and going while the brook flowed on for ever, as I did to Isaac Watts's Time, like an ever-rolling stream' bearing all its sons away.

My mother had a particular fondness for Tennyson's lyrics, and so did I, and so have I yet. The memorial on Tennyson Down on the Isle of Wight is, like Sway Tower, a landmark visible from the Solent and adjoining coastal area, so that, in time, I came to think of the great Victorian poet as somehow integral to the landscape, and not, as Auden wittily said, as a poet who had become a fossil on the Island! In this way, perhaps, I was able to bypass the modernist reaction against Tennyson. To me, long before, as a student, I worked as a deckhand on the Lymington – Yarmouth ferry during the summer vacations, and looked up at the evening star as I too crossed the bar, Tennyson was a living voice.

Another of his poems which, as a boy, I loved to hear was:

> Break, break, break
>   On thy cold grey stones, O sea!
> And I would that my tongue could utter
>   The thoughts that arise in me.

It may have been from this poem, I now realize, that I first derived my sense that poetry is about being inarticulate – that there is a silence below all words, which may be able to intimate what one thinks and feels, but cannot utter it.

Another poem which I loved to hear my mother recite was Southey's 'After Blenheim'. I was strangely excited and moved by the tale of the boy Peterkin, who finds a skull and takes it to his grandfather:

> ''Tis some poor fellow's skull', said he,
>   Who fell in the great victory.'

Since my grandfather had worked in the palace grounds, 'Blenheim' was, for me, a name which already had a ring to it. And, in those days, Peter was what I was called: it was my first name; soldiers billeted on us during the war, together with my brothers, had persuaded my parents that giving me only a 'soft' name like Jeremy would make me vulnerable to louts and bullies.

Skulls, too, fascinated me – they might have been the eggs of some prehistoric creature that had laid them in the chalk, but they were touched, also, by the darkness of mortality. These, of course, are later words, which attempt to evoke the beginnings of a literate and archaeological imagination. It wasn't that I was morbid, or more morbid than any sensitive child, but I did respond keenly to the elegiac note.

It was this that sounded in the men coming and going while the brook flowed on, in Time's ever-rolling stream, in the sea breaking on the cold grey stones, and, later, in the words spoken at the close of Evensong in Pennington Church, which made it my favourite service: 'O Lord, support us all the day long in this troublous life, until the shades lengthen, and the evening come, and the busy world is hushed, the fever of life is over and our work done…'

Later I tried to eradicate from myself the disposition to which such sentiments and cadences appealed. As a young man, during a bout of severe depression, I reacted violently against the elegiac. It seemed to me then like a disease imprinted in my very bones – not mine alone, but the bones of a people and a culture. It was as though English landscape, instead of affording a place to live, open to the future, weighed upon our spirit. Trapped inside myself, I heard the elegiac note in the sea breaking on the beach, outside the house where I was then living. Analysing it, as one does with deceptive and hopeless clairvoyance in the prison of depression, I saw sad nostalgia as both a disease and a cage, which English poetry reinforced. Desperate in my need, I sought to break out of the elegiac tradition, supporting myself in my efforts by turning to modern Welsh poetry, with its social and religious passion, and to American Black Mountain poetics.

I reasoned that there is something in English lyrical poetry, and especially in Tennysonian plangency and imagery of decay, that colludes with the spirit of imperial decline, and with an empty landscape, and the whole tendency – which George Orwell understood, from his own experience – for landscapes of childhood to become places of retreat, inner 'worlds', which afford an escape from a forbiddingly complicated present. If this is so, however, I can no more cease to love the poems my mother taught me than I can unknow them.

During the last year of her life, and again, in the last days, it was I who read to her, returning to Matthew Arnold's 'The Forsaken Merman', to William Barnes, and Robert Herrick, and Tennyson – to poems she could repeat in her mind, or whisper, but which I, with my poor memory, had to read. She only ever made one reference to her own coming death in my hearing, and that was on the day before she died, and I missed it. We would often swap quotations, and when she said to me: 'The best laid schemes o' mice an' men Gang aft a-gley', I responded by saying 'Robert Burns', to show that we were on the same wavelength. But at that moment, I later realized, we were not. She had been making schemes for the year ahead, and all the time becoming weaker, so that it was evident to everyone else that she was dying. And now, with a quotation, she acknowledged the fact, and I thought it was only another poetic reference.

My father began his working life as a gardener and in landscape gardening, and when he came to the south of England at the age of twenty-five, he was a sales representative for a seeds firm. This involved him in considerable travel, by car, between commercial growers and estates, mainly in Hampshire, Dorset and Wiltshire. I have a pocket edition of Hermann Lea's *Thomas Hardy's Wessex*, inscribed on the flyleaf: 'To My Own Dear Ivy. A Little Memento of my travels in Dorsetshire'. Aubrey's handwriting is bold and studied, similar to his father's copperplate – for both of them, the only tangible product of their schooling.

The wording and handwriting touch me more because I know the book was bought for Mother, not simply as a gift, but as a tribute to her as a reader, and as a sign to her that he was learning, was cultivating himself. The lovingly inscribed volume represents a small step in my parents' relationship.

When we first moved to Hayford, Northover Road had not been made up. It was a pot-holed, gravel cul de sac with six houses spaced out down one side, and two, including our house, on the other. The bungalow in which Charlie lived was diagonally across the road from Hayford, and next to it was a building site, or rather, a pile of bricks, which had stood there for some time, on ground which was going back to the wild, where there were slowworms, and lizards, and a bramble patch, from which, in the spring, we would hear nightingales singing at night. As on the Common, the more nervous among us trod cautiously in this place, in case we stepped on an adder. But the only adder I ever saw in the immediate area was a dead one, squashed flat, with a flattened frog, which it must have been swallowing, spread out in front of it, in the middle of Ramley Road and at the entrance to our lane.

Above Hayford, Northover Road became partially grass, and here I played cricket and football with Charlie and Robin Deacon, alongside a cow pasture, which was separated from the road by a barbed wire fence, and belonged to a farmer, Punch Browning, who lived in a house on the far side of the field, but in view of our games. He was quite a young man (as I see him now), but a frightening, red-faced tyrant, who swore at us when our ball landed among the cowpats in his field, and we crept under the fence to retrieve it. Northover Road still ends in a cul de sac, but the pasture has long since gone, and the area is now covered in bungalows and roads, including one called Browning's Close.

We did a lot of screaming in those days. It was most fun imitating the bloodcurdling yells of villains falling to their deaths as they tried to escape from Dick Barton, Special Agent, whose programmes I had Mother call me in to hear, every week-day evening at 6.45, when we were playing outside. The radio meant a lot to us in those days. I loved Children's Hour, and remember with affection the voices of Larry the Lamb and Denis the Dachshund, and the exciting adventures of Norman and Henry Bones the boy detectives. It must have been in this period, or perhaps a little later, that Dave and I tuned in breathlessly to each episode of *Journey into Space*, and shared the thrill of suspense as if we were boys together.

Robin Deacon was slightly older than Charlie and me, and always had the drop on us with his superior skill and cunning, whether we were playing cricket or football, or Cowboys and Indians, or conducting a race of woodlice on the concrete, garden path. What most impressed me about Robin, however, was his probity. I wouldn't have known the word then, but I was sensitive to his lessons in honesty, and to the shame of being found wanting. In the main, this involved owning up immediately when we were playing cricket, and the tennis ball touched the fruit crate which we used as a wicket. It would sometimes be possible to stand one's ground disputing the decision, since the bowler couldn't always prove that he had hit the crate. I tried this once, but Robin's reprimand cut so deeply into my conscience that, ever after, I would rather give myself out when I wasn't, than deny an appeal.

In my mind, the lesson of a moment – the hot blush of shame – is as tremendous as the time when I thought I might set the house on fire. We loved playing with matches, setting alight patches of dry grasses in the road, and watching them flare up. Once, practising this alone, on the hedge outside Hayford, the twigs and leaves caught, and, briefly, the fire flamed out of control, sending me into a panic in which I saw the house itself blazing, before I managed to stamp out the little fire. Other boys did set the Common on fire, especially every Bonfire Night, but the risk frightened me, and the destruction appalled. It was the coloured carcases of the dead fireworks that I loved to gather on the following morning, as much as the starbursts and whizzing catherine wheels and luminous smoke of the night before. The blackened bones of charred gorse have always seemed to me a most desolate thing.

To have gained so sharp an edge, Robin's lesson must have coincided with my first year at Rope Hill, the preparatory school to which my parents sent me, after my year at Rowan College. It was already their hope that, through education, I would fulfil the aspirations they had for me. No one on either side of the family had ever been to university, and Tony was a carpenter, and Dave, having left the RAF, was starting his training as a civil engineer. My parents had something else in mind for me – a degree, possibly followed by a teaching career – and they were prepared to spend some money on my education, instead of sending me to the local primary school. There was a time later when I wished passionately that they had. Then it seemed to me that I had been set apart from the friends that I most loved and admired – but that is not part of the story of my first twelve years.

I could describe Rope Hill, in retrospect, as a snob's academy. Once, walking in a crocodile of boys, I kicked a fir cone, and our teacher, Mr Randle, rebuked me, commenting that it was the secondary modern boys who did that sort of thing. On another occasion, in an attempt to reduce my Hampshire burr, I was given instructions in elocution, before being allowed to read one of the Christmas lessons, on behalf of the school, at Boldre Church. Warfare among the forty or so boys at Rope Hill took the form of running skirmishes between Conservative and Labour, the latter consisting of me, because my father was known to vote Labour, and Quentin Ralston, because his father was Russian.

It would be absurd, though, for me to write about Rope Hill as if it were some minor, provincial Eton, at which I had been scarified by the class system. Satire isn't in my line – I lack the aptitude and the appetite for it – and I'm no more at ease with knowing irony, which plays to a supposedly like-minded audience, and removes all chance of conveying a sense of original experience by replacing it with an adult perspective. I could say that, after five years at Rope Hill, I was ready to accede to the myth that they were the happiest days of my life. Happiness isn't the word, but it is probably better than any other.

For one thing, there was the cycle ride to school. All through country without much traffic on the roads at that time: from home along Ramley Road, past Morgan's Farm and Turville's Nursery, to The Wheel Inn. From the Wheel past Pardy's Farm, where I played cricket and football with Michael and Brian Pardy and other boys, in rough, cow pasture; by a hillocky meadow that was alive with rabbits; through Buckland Rings, a wooded prehistoric encampment, in which the one house then standing in the middle of the wood belonged to Colonel Impey, grandfather of a school friend, who, later, lent me his split cane fly-fishing rod. Coming out on the other side of the Rings, I took the road to Boldre, passing by the finest conker tree in the area, and fields beside the Lymington River, where, returning at evening, I would often see a barn owl as it followed the line of the river bank. The school, once, presumably, a gentleman's seat, stood in its own extensive, once landscaped, grounds on the hill above Boldre Bridge and the small village.

The educational aim of Rope Hill, as far as I can now see, was to equip us to enter the world as gentlemen – the 'world' being a minor public school, or (a step up from the secondary modern) Brockenhurst Grammar School, to which I would have gone eventually, if I hadn't twice failed the 11 plus. I was (and am) really very slow, with no aptitude for intelligence tests. So perhaps Rope Hill didn't do much for me, educationally.

What it did do was sharpen my already acute conscience to the point of near-madness. Decency and fair play and courtesy were instilled in us, until they became a skin, like the school uniform itself – the red cap with its distinctive long peak, which we were for ever raising to our elders, the red and grey blazer, the stag emblem on the cap and jacket pocket badges, the motto: *Nihil Nisi Optimum*.

Nothing but the best indeed. If a pupil committed a crime – not a misdemeanour, but a crime, such as the theft of a bicycle pump – I would agonize over whether I had done it, in a fit of absence of mind, and I suspect most of the other boys did too. Once we took a maths test, and at the end of it, the idea entered my head that my use of rough paper to work out the sums had been contrary to instructions, which I hadn't registered or understood. Tremulously, I held up my hand: 'Please, sir, I think I've cheated'.

Mr Randle was the teacher from whom I learnt most at Rope Hill. In my mind's eye, he is a well-built man of above average height in his late twenties or early thirties; he wears his thinning, fair hair combed across his round head, and he looks at us with an ironic smile, through a pair of gold-rimmed spectacles. He wears a gold ring on one of his plump fingers; his fingernails are well-manicured. Everything about his appearance and dress is redolent of his love of music, acting and literature, and bespeaks 'culture'. Dave would have hated him. He has a humorous way of dealing with inattentive or misbehaving boys, which involves pulling them about the classroom, in and out of the legs supporting the blackboard, by their hair, or hurling a board-rubber, which bounces off wall or desk with a resounding thwack. In consequence, there is little mischief in his classes. There is a twinkle of ironic amusement about his eyes, except when he speaks to us, with real distaste, of 'Randy' Turpin, the boxer, then in the news, and apparently the only famous contemporary to come from Mr Randle's home town.

It was from Mr Randle that I learnt of the existence of modern poetry. He once read us one of his own poems, and was disappointed by our response. His poem featured a blue jay, and, with my interest in and knowledge of British birds, I had the nerve to tell him there was no such thing. He may have been referring to the American variety of course, but I suspect that my know-all response had some truth to it, and he had found his blue jay in a book, not in a tree.

One poem he read to us was Stephen Spender's 'The Pylons', whose 'pillars/Bare like nude giant girls' became for me, for a time, the very spirit of modern verse. He read to us from *Under Milk Wood* also, and my memory pictures him reading the strange and magical words *from a newspaper*, in which the poem or an extract from it was printed. Is that possible, I wonder? At any rate, the idea that daring new poetry is *news* was accentuated for me by the mental picture of Mr Randle reading Dylan Thomas from a newspaper.

> It is spring, moonless night in the small town, starless
> and bible-black, the cobblestones silent and the hunched,
> courters'-and-rabbits' wood limping invisible down to the
> sloeback, slow, black, crowblack, fishingboat-bobbing sea.

Mr Randle paused after reading this passage, spelling words for us, in the hope that we would get the point of the verbal trickery. I don't know how the other boys felt – to my knowledge, their interest in poetry matched their sympathy for Labour politics – but for me something new entered the world, something rich and strange, which contrasted (though I would not have been able to articulate this then) with the austere spirit of the times.

Apart from the cultured Mr Randle Rope Hill didn't offer a rich educational experience. Several of the teachers were ex-Army majors and the like, decent, conscientious men, but more inclined to hold forth on personal obsessions – one knew all about steam locomotives – than to inform us of things that would help us to pass exams. But in any case, I was not very bright.

Yet this was only true as far as 11-plus type mental efficiency was concerned. Something was happening to me at Rope Hill that was different from my experience at the schools which I had previously attended. From Miss Wemys's, I remember reading aloud, and drawing fighter planes, and, once, to Miss Wemys's indignation and disgust, being sick all over the classroom table. From St Nicholas's, I could still hear the voices of two young women teachers, addressing me in unison: 'Stop giggling; we don't like little boys who giggle'. (From that rebuke, which humiliated and bewildered me, dates, perhaps, my recurring sense that I was not a likeable little boy.) At Rope Hill, however, despite Mr Valentine, I was beginning to be recognised as a person.

On one peculiar occasion, when I was playing the fool, the teacher reprimanded me: 'You should know better, Hooker, after all you're supposed to be the most intelligent boy in the class'. I was embarrassed but also gratified, and, most of all, astonished. But the idea lodged in my mind – perhaps there was more to me than my blank stare at a problem in geometry, indeed at the very phenomenon of geometry, would suggest.

At the same time, I was developing emotionally. At Rope Hill I formed a passionate attachment to a boy called Peter, who, intermittently, returned my friendship. He was small and compact, good looking, witty, and good at sports. I was big and slow, with a dreamy, unformed look (as photographs testify), and tended to be inarticulate, except on paper. Once Peter and I were sharing a changing cubicle at Lymington Baths, when Matron walked in without knocking. Seeing the door open and thinking it was another boy coming to claim our space, I bawled: 'Get out!' I apologized profusely to Matron, of course, and was alarmed that, instead of letting the matter drop, as the genuine mistake it was, Matron and the Headmaster both questioned me closely, as if something other than changing into swimming trunks – but what? – had been going on in the cubicle.

More self-confidence came during my five years at Rope Hill, mainly through my achievements at cricket, and especially through my ability to bowl, which made me a hero in that small world. The gift was untaught, instinctual – one day, at Rowan College, I found myself wheeling my arm over, and bowling effectively. At Rope Hill, I became the star bowler, taking an average of five wickets per match. My greatest triumph occurred in a match with Walhampton School, when, with the first two balls of my opening over, full-length onto the batsmen's pads, I had the first and third batsman out LBW, and went on to take 8 for 12. It was the stuff of comic book or *Boy's Own* romance, and I see myself, as in a cartoon, blown up to a bladder of pride, but appearing extremely modest.

Cricket, in any case, was a game that I loved. Tom and Aubrey had both played for Sarisbury Green, and Tom was said to have played with Lord Tennyson. My father spoke reverently of Hedley Verity and Phil Mead – figures on cigarette cards to me – and Len Hutton, who was one of my heroes too, although the only time I saw him play, he was out first ball.

Cricket became an important element in my fantasy life as well as in fact. I played endless games of paper cricket, invented a winning team made up of friends and imaginary characters, in which I was the star batsman and bowler, and spent hours bouncing a tennis ball off the house wall, and catching it, with acrobatic leaps, on the lawn – Out! Not out! Four! Six! Sadly for me, though, my gift deserted me as mysteriously as it had come.

Do we remember humiliation and embarrassments and failures, much better than successes, not because we are humble, but because we are proud? Is one's 'name' an invisible balloon, which goes sailing around the world, vulnerable to any criticism or suspected slight, when it is we who feel the sharp prick, and are deflated? My father, in his 90s, remembering a working visit to an estate in Dorset, recalled the impatient word a young woman had spoken to him, and smarted. In his mind, he would be again a little boy, hurt and outraged by his father's lack of understanding. Time, it seems, doesn't exist in the mind, especially as far as our humiliations are concerned.

There are memories of long ago which, even now, when they suddenly come into my mind, make me duck, as if warding off an invisible blow, and shout out. One of them concerns a game of cricket.

Great success in the tiny cricketing world of Rope Hill led to an arrangement for me to be coached by professional county players at the Hampshire County Cricket ground at Bournemouth, in the year in which I left Rope Hill. I would travel down in the bus with Donald Whitlock, who was a fine young cricketer; but already other interests were absorbing my attention, and what I noticed most, on the bus journey, were the moist, new leaves – the different leaves – on the trees, which brushed against the upper deck windows. Already, then, I felt a current of new, strong feeling.

Maybe that had something to do with my loss of cricketing ability – at any rate, it deserted me. One day John Arlott, paying a visit to his HCC friends, bowled at me in the nets – slow left arm flighted deliveries – and, to my shame, I couldn't lay a bat on them. I admired John Arlott – years later, when I was living away from Hampshire, his voice on the radio was the voice of home to me. When I published my first book of poems, he wrote a kind review of it for *The Hampshire Magazine*. Writing to thank him, I recalled the hopelessly incompetent youngster he had bowled to in the nets.

I had never been much use with a bat anyway, but now I had lost my ability to bowl. This didn't become fully evident to me until I played with a team of strangers, at the cricket ground at Pennington, and the captain, having heard of my reputation, asked me to open the bowling. I did, with six slow dolly drops that the opening batsmen hit all round the ground. This, however, wasn't the worst of it.

I was wearing my father's old cricket flannels, and only noticed, when in the middle, that they had a long yellow piss stain round the crotch and down the leg. This, I tried to persuade myself, really looked green, and would be taken for a grass stain. Nevertheless, I tried to conceal it as well as I could by pulling down my white jersey as far as it would go, and, whenever possible, holding my hands crossed on my leg, and standing at angles to players and spectators. The result was a mounting self-consciousness, and I would have squirmed into the ground like a worm if I could. Coming in for tea, with my hands held in front of me, I met the appraising stare of Ros Gunnell, an older local girl who liked nothing more than insulting boys, and who saw me, no doubt, as stuck up and wet. 'You can't hide it, you know,' she said in a loud mocking voice. And as, to my ears, her words echoed round the ground, I knew that I had been exposed – a beanpole of a youth who should have bowled like a demon, but was really only an overgrown baby who still pissed in his pants.

Rugby and football matches were usually miserable affairs at Rope Hill, since oppositions from bigger schools routinely crushed us. Our solitary hero was a large, strong boy – a handsome giant in my eyes – called Palmer, whose father was a Gurkha. Palmer simply ran through opposing teams, brushing them off; but ultimately to little purpose, since no one was capable of following him. He impressed me deeply with his combination of physical power, gentleness and integrity, and I knew that he impressed Mr Bullard, our Sunday School teacher at Pennington, too. Lacking Palmer's all round sporting prowess, the best I could hope for was that Rope Hill would turn me out as what a Tom Stoppard character calls 'one of life's cricketers'.

25 November

As I left the house for my morning walk, Joan came out of her bungalow across the road to speak to me. She wanted to know how Mieke was, and

I was able to say a little better. Tall, gaunt and bronchitic, Joan has been suffering from the same virus, and is still unwell. But her eyes sparkled when she told me that, yesterday afternoon, she had had a surprise visit from her nephew, formerly a soldier in Germany, and his family.

On my walk, I noticed that moisture had brought out a large number of worms, which were at full stretch, long sensitive organs of the earth itself, on the damp, tarmacadam path. I always wonder why they do it. It's such a risk, as one sees from the number of dead or dying worms left on paths which the sun has dried; and why should the soil be more nutritious on one side of a path rather than the other? I have a guilty affection for these creatures, from the days when I impaled them on hooks; and they call to mind one of my favourite passages in William Blake's prose, in which he says God 'is become a worm that he may nourish the weak'. Now that I walk slowly, I have literally come closer to a child's perspective again, with my eyes on the ground.

James Wood, in his elegant book of essays on literature and belief, *The Broken Estate*, says:

> Life-under-God seems a pointlessness posing as a purpose (the purpose, presumably, being to love God and to be loved in return); life-without-God seems to me also a pointlessness posing as a purpose (jobs, family, sex and so on – all the usual distractions). The advantage, if it can be described as one, of living in the later state, without God, is that the false purpose has at least been invented by man, and one can strip it away to reveal the *actual* pointlessness.

Intellectually, I can see that this could be the reaction of a mind which has rejected the claims of evangelical Christianity to absolute truth and adopted its negation. But I find it very difficult to accept that anyone could really believe that life is pointless.

To my mind and feeling, the point of life is life itself. I don't mean some notion of life-force, but the lives of actually existing beings, more specifically, the unique life of each.

The truth of this was revealed to me by my own destructive acts. Once I killed a bumble bee by swiping it out of the air with a tennis racket. On another occasion, out with a friend who was shooting at things with an airgun, I asked to have a shot. He gave me the gun, and I levelled it at a sparrow pecking on the gravel in a neighbouring garden and pulled the trigger. To my amazement (for I had never fired a gun before) the sparrow dropped dead. One moment it was full of life, the next it was as dead as the stones where it lay. I had always been horrified by cruelty – boys ragging birds-nests, or putting live fish on the road for cars to run over, or swinging green crabs on fishing lines, hard against the seawall – but it wasn't these instances, or even the knowledge of my own capacity for cruelty, that horrified me most. It was the thought that that particular bumble bee and that particular sparrow would *never* live again, however many other bumble bees and sparrows would come into existence.

The thought of these creatures probably helped to make me more conscious of the uniqueness of individual beings, which, to my feeling, is the point of human life. The awareness had fully dawned when I agonized over the execution of Derek Bentley, and the deaths of the Manchester United players in the Munich air disaster, seeing their faces and silently naming them over and over again, filled with horror and pity at the thought that they could never be brought back again. It wasn't that I was more sensitive to injustice or tragedy than any other boy; I was even perhaps rather insensitive in thinking far less of the mourners. What haunted me was the thought that each of those men had had his life taken away – it was the unique, the irreplaceable, that bit into my heart and mind.

Of course, we do not know with absolute certainty that individual being – the soul – is extinguished. All that we can be sure of is the silence and emptiness afterwards: the *not here*. It doesn't seem to me that meaning – the point of life – is a given absolute. My feeling, rather, is that each one of us carries, with his or her uniqueness, the question of meaning. If I have understood him correctly, James Wood is offering an answer: 'the *actual* pointlessness' of 'life-without-God'. From where I stand, the certainty of this seems like a kind of bravado. As far as God is concerned, if it makes any sense to *talk* about God at all, I prefer the image of Blake's worm nourishing the weak. Rather than having an answer, I feel that each human being is the question, and the question – and how each lives the question – is the meaning.

But I can't rest on any formulation, and the neater it is, the less I can abide it. That which is unique is beyond all formulations, all images, all words – the most one can do is constantly make new beginnings, hoping always to get a little closer. One day, when I was sitting beside him in the nursing home, my father stunned me. Suddenly, without any preamble, in a wondering, bemused tone of voice, he spoke: 'Aubrey Hooker, that was his name'. It was as if, in his blindness, he was seeing himself for the first time – seeing himself, not from within his life, but from outside: as though he were already dead, but somehow conscious, looking at the man he had been. This strange and poignant event shook me, and disturbed my sense of the continuity of personal existence. I felt that one might look at oneself as though one were an effigy, or a husk which no longer contained one's being, or a name one did not possess, was no longer inside of. What had I seen and heard? A stage in the dissolution of personal identity; or an affirmation made on the verge of the grave? Now, when I look at my father's signature, in the bottom left hand corner of his paintings, I hear him speak those words.

My fascination with fishing began in unfortunate circumstances.

An older boy at Rope Hill, with whom I had occasionally gone sailing together with his parents and sister, in their small yacht, on the Solent, asked me to go on holiday with them. His best friend, who usually accompanied them on holiday, was ill, so I went as the replacement, as it were, to a caravan park on the cliffs above Durdle Door in Dorset.

From the beginning, the holiday was a disaster. David was an active, outgoing, adventurous boy, who wanted to scramble up and down cliffs, swim, sail. I was mesmerized by the deep water off the rocks, by the anglers' red floats bobbing on the surface, by rock pools, and, when we went sailing, by the water beside the boat. I spent most of the time wishing that I, too, had a fishing rod, and watching and watching as the floats bobbed up and down and went under, and the anglers reeled in brightly coloured wrasse.

David soon let me know that he disliked me, and I was ruining his holiday. The adults silently communicated their dislike for the quiet, moon-eyed, introspective boy, who was acting unnaturally, not as a boy should. I felt guilty and miserable, and wore my stoic face. And the time passed – the weeks – and I longed to be at home with my dog. Boxer was a cross between a Boxer and a Golden Labrador; I had had him since he was a puppy, and at that time he was my best friend. We would set out early in the morning to hunt rabbits in the long grass of the Park or among gorse bushes on Pennington Common, and we both got very excited when a rabbit popped out of grass or bush, and he chased it, hopelessly. When he was older he did actually catch one – a big, pop-eyed rabbit dying from myxomatosis, which I took from him, and killed. Due to lack of training, he was a badly behaved dog, all wild good-nature – once I took him on the bus to Rope Hill, and we joined a school nature excursion in fields by the Lymington River, where he went completely out of control. We all, boys and master, chased him, getting wet and muddy, and when I went home on the bus, tired and wet, with a wet dog, I was very happy.

Eventually the nightmare holiday ended, and I came home to Boxer. I brought the obsession with fishing with me, and was soon sitting beside the old bridge at Wainsford, fishing with some thread line attached to a bamboo pea-stick out of the garden, and using bread paste on the hook. Almost contrary to the law of nature – though I didn't know it then – I caught not one but six trout, each 2 or 3 ounces in weight, but big compared to minnows, and to me big fish.

And so the love affair began. Weekend by weekend, holiday by holiday, over the next few years, I went fishing. For trout and sea-trout in the Avon Water, at Wainsford and along Wainsford Common, at Gordleton Mill and Flexford Mill and Mead End; in the Lymington River, at Boldre, and at Brockenhurst, in the New Forest. For coarse fish in the lakes belonging to the once-great estates in the area, at Newlands Manor (where in memory I see big golden carp leaping into the air and falling in a curve back into the water with a mighty splash), at Walhampton and Pylewell; occasionally in the great hammerpond at Sowley, and in long Hatchet Pond, once a gravel pit, a sheet of water on the bleak heathland towards Beaulieu. Here, the water was in places so deep it was said to be bottomless, and I and my fishing friends believed the tale that a German plane had gone down in the pond during the war, and never been found. We thought the pilot's ghost haunted the place, and, fishing late, the hair on the backs of our heads would bristle as we looked across the water at the group of Scots pines standing in dusky shadows on the farther bank. I was rarely bored when fishing, but do recall one occasion, under this same group of pines, when, at the end of a day without a bite, Nick Craze and I fought by hurling dried pony dung at each other.

I developed skills appropriate to different kinds of fishing – with float, and fly, and ledger for carp and tench, at dawn and nightfall, in the lakes. I took *The Angling Times* from the first issue, and fell under the spell of Bernard Venables' purple prose, and became interested in technicalities, through the austere, practical articles of Dick Walker. I bought a copy of Bernard Venables' *Mr Crabtree Goes Fishing*, and identified with the boy, Peter, whose father teaches him how to catch every species of freshwater fish (and they always do catch them!), and imitated Venables' drawings. I read and reread Arthur Ransome's *With Rod and Line* and BB's *Confessions of a Carp Fisher*. I went sea-fishing, too, off the beach at Milford and Hordle and Barton, at Hurst shingle-spit and among the mudflats on its near side, where one looks across marshes and down the Solent, past mast-forests at Keyhaven and Lymington, towards Southampton Water. I went night fishing off Hurst Castle with a friend, in the deep called The Hole, just off the beach, where, at high water, we caught bass and conger eels and small pout-whiting. And when the tide turns, the ebb runs like a train, and even a heavy lead weight will be carried rapidly down channel, pulling line off the reel and making the ratchet scream. One night, as we were fishing with our backs to the castle, where Charles I had been imprisoned before being taken to London and executed, we told each other silly stories about his headless ghost; and a huge roller of black cloud began to move over the open sea, beyond West Wight and the Needles, bearing down on us. And now we told a more frightening story, that this was a tidal wave, a huge, slow-moving tidal wave, which would engulf the castle and the shingle-spit; and, quickly and clumsily, we dismantled our rods and packed our tackle, and walked, as quickly as we could, the whole length of the shingle-spit, back to Saltgrass Lane, where we had left our bikes, the mass of shifting small stones grabbing at our ankles.

During my first weeks in hospital, when I couldn't sit up or get out of bed without help, I thought the thing I most wanted to do was go fishing. And I imagined myself sitting on a rock, somewhere in the West Country, fishing in the sea. The fact that I wouldn't then have been able to sit on a rock made the idea especially attractive. The past was coming back to me, in mind-bubbles, like the bubbles carp make, near lily pads, when mist is rising from still lake water at dawn in June. I recalled a mellow day in September at Rat Island, a place that is only an island when the tide is in, on the estuarine side of the Hurst shingle-spit. It is a mound of broken bricks – remnants of a wartime defensive position – and seaweedy stones, the higher part a soft patch of grass and thrift. In the salt water off Rat Island I would catch flounders and checker bass, or small green crabs, or nothing. On this particular day I lay on my back on the grass and watched clouds floating over on the blue sky – ribbed clouds that look like slow-moving, white sand-banks – and what I knew was perfect happiness – now, this day, and all the days to come, a procession of days as endless as the sky, no end in sight to me of days fishing at Rat Island.

It is that being in life which is impossible to recapture, the one thing that really matters, the only thing that exists, the living moment. In recollection, one is outside, seeing oneself, as I see myself lying on my back looking at the sky. But it was contactual knowledge that came to me in fishing, not external views, but intimate knowledge of the ways of water, hollows under tree roots where the bigger trout were, deeper slack water beside or at the tail of a current, where fish would wait for food, the still reach under a bridge that would hold a cannibal trout, runnels between weed-beds, skitterings on the surface, subtle dimples under the farther bank. Water slowly turning in a pool is the old hypnotist, inducing a dream in which the mind too slowly revolves, but I learnt also to read what was happening in the dark, where the underwater tongues probe and excavate, or at least to read partially, sensing the hidden world. And as I learnt to read water for the signs of fish, so I went in search of new waters. I would pour over maps, and go for long cycle rides into the New Forest. On one excursion with a friend, looking through the trees, we simultaneously saw the same thing – a long stretch of beautiful green water – and jumped off our bikes and threw them down beside the road, and ran through the trees towards the lake. And when we came near to it, saw that it was a lawn, as areas of close cropped grass are called in the Forest.

In hospital, I saw again years of days, early mornings and evenings: a bitter hour in February when I cried with cold, but still fished on; a storm in which rain ran down the back of my neck and soaked every part of my body; an April morning, when white windflowers were out under the oak trees beside the Lymington River, between Balmer Lawn and Queens Bower, when I should have been so happy … But I could probably no more fish now than I could go back, for I have grown more tender-minded, less able to overlook how a stabbed worm or a hooked fish feels, for certainly they do feel, though the dream figure which I had despatched to sit on a rock had no more wanted to know that, than I did when I was a boy.

Memory is a trickster, of course. I recall my contemptuous laugh of agreement when my fishing friend, Rod Saunders, spoke scornfully of a slightly older acquaintance who no longer had money to spend on fishing tackle, because he was spending it on 'girls'. Yet, surely, by that time, I myself was no longer immune.

Other boys I knew had sisters. I didn't, and I felt my lack keenly, especially after we left Warsash, and I no longer played with my cousins, Christine and Janet. Like most children, I had told myself stories from an early age, and looked forward to going to bed so that I could continue an endless serial adventure. Now, I invented a sister. Adopted would be more accurate. Early issues of the new comic, *Eagle*, which had educational aims distinguishing it from *Beano* and *Dandy*, which I also bought with my pocket money, when I could afford to, carried a serial story in pictures on the back cover. This was about the life of St Patrick, who had a beautiful, black-haired sister. I don't remember her name now, but for a time she became my fantasy sister, and played a leading part in stories in which I cast myself in a protective role, as her daring rescuer from many dangers. In the *Eagle* series, her fate was martyrdom, which I couldn't bear to contemplate. As I recall, my name for her was Pat.

A year or so later, I acquired a second sister, Sally, who was slight and fair-haired, in contrast to the more statuesque Pat. Sally materialised during my first visit to Wales, at Builth Wells, when I spent a wet week fishing in the flooded Wye, and met 'Sally' on the stairs of our hotel, a young newlywed, with her corduroy-jacketed husband, who didn't interest me at all.

There was nothing incestuous about these imaginary relationships. They were highly idealized, and provided me with the companionship of witty and attractive sisters, in whose eyes I could play the part of hero. This, indeed, seems to have been their main function, since, for them, I transformed myself from a gangling, mouse-haired, dreamy-eyed boy into a dashing, handsome figure with jet-black hair.

From remarks that Mother made late in life to my wife, I know that she and Father knew nothing about sex when they were first married. They were always extremely reticent on the subject. During the Builth Wells holiday my mother tried to warn me, awkwardly, about 'homosexuals'. I didn't know what she was talking about, and assumed she meant my friend, David Hayter, because he had told me the little I knew about sex.

David's teachings had been lessons in lust, and they coincided with the physical changes that I would later know as puberty. At the time I didn't know what was happening, and in consequence thought that I alone, in all the world, harboured lustful desires for older girls and women, including several of my friends' mothers. Moreover, I knew nothing about the physiology of sex and little about sexual differences. On one excursion to Hurst Castle, I had caught sight of a young girl's body below the waist, as she was drying herself with a towel after swimming, and felt, with horror and pity, that she had suffered a terrible accident. When Tony's first child was born, a daughter, I asked, in a room full of adults, how one could tell the difference between boy and girl babies. He handled the situation well, saying it was something to do with the colour of the hair, then took me aside to ask whether I really didn't know.

Knowing nothing about the physiology of sex, I believed that conception occurred through the penis being pressed against the breast, via the nipple. Deliberately recalling this and the incident at Julie's christening,

I go hot and cold with embarrassment – they are among the memories which, springing unexpectedly into my mind, over the years, have made me duck my head, and shout out. But if I am to recapture anything of the sensation of life, I have to record them.

My lust seemed to me completely unnatural, and sinful. At that time, I had a strong sense of sin, which was a product of my religious upbringing. In my own small way, I seem even to have re-enacted the story of Eve plucking the apple from the Tree of the Knowledge of Good and Evil. On a trestle in the garden at Fairacre, a fine tomato was ripening in advance of all the rest. In no circumstances was I to pick it, my parents commanded. So I looked at it and looked at it, and, as the snowman had once spoken in my head, telling me to run away from home, so the Devil urged me; and I picked the fruit.

Tormented by lustful thoughts, I was not only a sinner, but the only sinner – a lost soul. There was no human being I could talk to, or so I felt. And now my first depression began, which, inevitably, I came afterwards to associate with sexual guilt.

I say first depression, but that isn't how anyone regards such an experience. At the time, it is an absolute condition, all-absorbing, a black inner weather that seems to come from nowhere, and to be for always. One doesn't think of it, in childhood, as a first occasion which will be followed by others, or as 'depression'. It is simply feeling – a sick emptiness that is somehow full, like black rainwater filling a rotten tree stump (so I have come to see it as an adult), and it pervades one's whole being. It was there when I got up in the morning, and when I cycled to Rope Hill (at this time constantly looking down in case my fly buttons were undone), and when I sat in class, and when I cycled home. Even when I went fishing, walking along the riverbank under the oaks at Brockenhurst, in April when the white anemones were in flower, it was inside me, as though I myself were the rotten tree stump. It took all my control, all my stoicism, not to betray its existence with any emotional sign. Intensely secretive, and feeling worthless, I began to think about suicide. It is impossible for me now to know how serious this was – not my philosophy only, but my very feeling, most of the time, is 'the pleasure which there is in life itself'. All I know is that I became obsessed with the idea of obtaining a revolver, with which I would shoot myself.

Not any gun – had that been the aim, I might have been able to get hold of the gun with which my friend Nick Craze went out shooting pigeons and rooks. And not any other means of putting an end to myself.

I didn't know why, and, more than likely, I didn't want to.

What I longed for was oblivion. And in this crisis, which lasted about a year, and was followed by an almost equally distressing period of blankness, of feeling nothing, the only peace I found was, in a way, religious. It is hard for me to say this, even to myself, harder even than to embarrass myself with recollections of sexual ignorance. But there it is – religion, now, is the greater embarrassment.

During this period, I prayed. It wasn't so much prayer, as generally understood, as conversation – not dialogue, because I received no verbal answer, but not monologue either, because I felt I was listened to. The person I addressed was 'Lord' – an idea of Jesus Christ, I would now say, as real to me as Pat and Sally; not the tortured figure of Christian iconography, nor the creeping Jesus which I associated, unkindly, with Aunty May, but an all-understanding friend – someone more like Tony or David, but with knowledge and understanding far greater than theirs.

Where did this presence come from? I was brought up in the Church of England and religion was as integral to our way of life as school was. I went to church as a matter of course, and the language of the services and the hymns became part of my mind. I neither doubted nor assented to religious belief until I was in my teens, any more than I thought about what composed the air I breathed. The Pennington vicar of that time gave me few incentives to piety. He was a burly, red-haired man, with whom I played cricket for the village. He was imperious, and bad-tempered when given out to what he regarded as a dubious decision, and when one dropped a catch off his bowling, as I once did. I recall pep talks in church, which involved hints about self-abuse (I knew what it was by then) and confirmation classes, which I remember for a black-haired fellow communicant whom I adored. What I also remember is an occasion when the vicar mentioned the word *pilgrim*, and David Hayter whispered in my ear, *grimpil*, which was the first of many times when church-going became synonymous for me with agonies of rocking or holding myself rigid in the pew to stop myself bursting with laughter. But, for all that I shall never be able to hear the word *pilgrim* without laughing, the simple interior of St Mark's Church, Pennington, with its gaudy stained glass windows and brass wall plaques commemorating the dead of the world wars, is a sacred place for me.

My parents were religious, in a non-emphatic way. But probably the greatest influence on me in that respect as a boy was Mr Bullard. Mr Bullard must have been in his sixties when I first encountered him, and I came to see him, over the years, as one of the old men of the village – men who have disappeared now, but who were venerable figures in the rural England of my boyhood. Mr Bullard was tall and upright, and always dressed in a dark business suit and wore shining black boots. He lived with an invalid wife, caring for her and doing the housework, in their cottage on Wainsford Common, which looked downhill over the gorse to where willows and thorns and brambles hid the course of Avon Water. He walked everywhere, with his soldierly gait, and was often to be seen crossing the commons on his way to or from Lymington. On Sunday mornings, he taught a group of us – 6 or 7 boys – in the vestry of St Mark's.

There were aspects of Mr Bullard which, as I recall them now, may make him seem absurd, though he was a man I shall always revere. His was a fiercely puritanical, Christian spirit. As an officer in the trenches during the First World War, he had waged a campaign against the men's use of profane language, of what David Jones called 'the efficacious word'. Having taken *Ulysses* out of Lymington library and read it, he tried to have the book removed from the shelves. We didn't know enough to see the absurdity in this side of his behaviour when we were boys, and I doubt that any of us now, in later middle age, would remember Mr Bullard without affection, and above all, respect.

He was a formidable figure, and we were in awe of him. If any boy distracted him with inappropriate behaviour (no sniggering over *grimpils* in his classes) – the offender was, not infrequently, Johnny Norman – he would dismiss him from the room with an explosion of fury that left the rest of us white-faced and shaking. Once we watched transfixed, unable to speak or make any sign, as a sleepy red admiral butterfly, woken from hibernation among priestly vestments, crawled over Mr Bullard's boot, up his black sock, and, with agonizing slowness, onto the white of his exposed skin, and disappeared up his trouser leg. He talked to us about different things, including the insurance business, and his experience as a young man of challenging atheist speakers to debate at Hyde Park Corner, making them interesting, and, whatever the subject, conveying a powerful sense of Christian morality and integrity. In all he did and said, Mr Bullard, was a man who, not as a representative of church or state, but in himself, had authority.

Mr Bullard was kind to me, and I shall always think of him as one of the few truly good men it has been my privilege to meet. But I have to say this also: with his example added to the other manly influences upon me, and with my religious background and the determination of Rope Hill to make me a gentleman, it was a terrible thing to find myself, at the age of 11, the only sinner in the world.

I would dearly love to be able to remember the sequence or coincidence of events during the onset of puberty. For it doesn't seem credible to me that the year of black misery could have overlapped with the time when I first became conscious of nature, which I remember for its ecstasy. Yet I feel that those experiences must have coincided to some degree – and perhaps this makes sense, for the ecstatic temperament is especially prone to darker emotions.

Despite the fluency with which I could read, I was not one of those prodigies who has read the classics of English literature by the age of twelve. Indeed the only thing that was prodigious about me was my slowness. I was what was called a slow-developer, and, in accordance with my belief in constant new beginnings, I still am. By the age of twelve I had read all the William books and most of the Biggles books, and the epic tale of a man and a dog called *Finn the Wolfhound*, which I found in the Rope Hill library; it is the only novel which I have ever read over and over again, beginning again at the beginning each time I reached the end.

At about the age of twelve, however, an event which was to shape my writing life occurred, when I took a green-covered book, *Jefferies' England*, from my parents' bookcase, and started to read Richard Jefferies's essays. Almost immediately, I began to see the world around me with Jefferies's eyes. Previously I had enjoyed an active country boyhood, fishing, playing, hunting rabbits with Boxer, finding sweet chestnuts and conkers, birds-nesting. I was proud of my ability to find birds' nests, apparently having an instinct for where they were, and detecting them in the densest bushes and hedgerows. But I hadn't really *seen* them, or any other natural objects, before I looked with Jefferies's eyes.

Reading Jefferies helped to awaken me to the world around me, to trees and flowers and birds, not to the appearance of things only, but to the life in them, to that which gives a branching oak tree, for example, its extraordinary shape, and makes it at once quintessentially oak, and different from any other oak tree. Travelling with Donald Whitlock on the bus to Bournemouth, I was seeing the May leaves as I had never seen them before, all the varied leaves on different trees, with a sappy greenness, which was colour that flowed in them.

Jefferies could be a sentimental writer, especially in the late essays which he wrote (or dictated to his wife) when he was in pain, and knew that he was dying: a life-worshipper acutely conscious of failing vital power.

His pathetic note was partly what appealed to me then; it was a personal poignancy, combined with the art of seeing life in common things; an art whose intimacy paradoxically coincided with his distance from nature, and his isolation.

It was passages such as this from 'Hours of Spring' that so moved me:

> The green hawthorn buds prophesy on the hedge; the reed pushes up in the moist earth like a spear thrust through a shield; the eggs of the starling are laid in the knot-hole of the pollard elm – common eggs, but within each a speck that is not to be found in the cut diamond of two hundred carats – the dot of protoplasm, the atom of life. There was one row of pollards where they always began laying first. With a big stick in his beak the rook is blown aside like a loose feather in the wind; he knows his building-time from the fathers of his house – hereditary knowledge handed down in settled course; but the stray things of the hedge, how do they know? … I think of the drift of time, and I see the apple bloom coming and the blue veronica in the grass. A thousand thousand birds and leaves and flowers and blades of grass, things to note day by day, increasing so rapidly that no pencil can put them down and no book can hold them, not even to number them – and how to write the thoughts they give? All these without me – how can they manage without me?

The images make this one of Jefferies' poetic passages. Almost equally attractive to me were those in which he noted some unregarded ditch or field corner, revealing the value above price of common places. But here, in this passage, Jefferies shows himself; his inarticulacy at the thoughts which nature gives, his anguish at the perception that nature can get along perfectly well without him. It is a vision of nature's abundant riches and of the writer's contrasting poverty; but the writing is not poor in expression. On the contrary, it has something of the emotion of great love poetry, which expresses a hopeless passion, and the poet's inability to do justice to the object of his love. It is vulnerable writing, of course; no writing could be otherwise, which attempts to convey the quick of life as it flows.

As a writer who captures the sensation of life, Jefferies means as much to me now as he did when I was twelve. But, looking again at a passage such as this, I realise the special appeal which he had for me then, as I entered upon puberty. The poignant personal note speaks to the isolation that one first knows with the consciousness of separation from the world one has been part of. The seeing that accompanies it is ecstatic – the branchy oaks, the green light in the leaves – and touched with melancholy. Love and desire both come with distance, as primary attachments loosen, and one sees people and things that are not oneself. And now, too, desire may separate from love, becoming lust. Where life had flowed holding you, more or less, within it, there were now whirlpools and eddies and turbulent cross-currents, and you were both tossed about among them and could see yourself, an isolated figure. So it seems to me anyway, as I reread Jefferies, and look back to the period in my life when I first read him.

There are, it seems to me now, an erotic element in Jefferies's art of seeing, and a knowledge of death. Without these, no ecstasy, no melancholy. You know now that the life you love will go on without you, and that it always does anyway. What is knowledge but nature's gift of death? Could we think anything at all without nature? We love it in our need, selfishly. But the possibility dawns of loving it for itself, even as we know we will be dispensed with.

From Jefferies's essays it was a step to Thomas Hardy's novels. But this occurred for me as I was leaving Rope Hill, which is where the part of this story concerning my early years ends. It was Jefferies who showed me where I was living – the life of the immediate area, and the surrounding woods and fields and commons and waters.

From about this time I remember a number of external events: being taken 'to review the fleet' – sea battleship-grey below a tilting deck – at Portsmouth; going in a school party to see *The Ascent of Everest* at the Lyric Cinema in Lymington; watching the Coronation on a TV set belonging to a wealthy neighbour, with my father and mother and my brother David, and the neighbours' family, his daughter's hair brushing my face like a feather. I recall also an open-air production of *Much Ado About Nothing* in the Cloisters at Beaulieu Abbey, which I enjoyed, but sat through being tormented by gnats and feeling humiliated, because I was still wearing short trousers, and the other prefects from Rope Hill had their legs covered up by long grey flannels. The Abbey comes back to me also, from a time long before the Motor Museum, as a stretch of broken, grey stone wall, which I explore, perfectly alone, finding the broken shell of a pigeon's egg in a dusty crevice. I am alone because my father has taken me with him in the car, on one of his visits – this, perhaps, was the time when he was advising on the vineyard that was being established at Beaulieu. He liked my company; later, I realized that he needed it. Often I would sit in the car, sketching what I could see through the window – a wall, a ditch, a tree. In retrospect I have sometimes associated these visits with an emptiness, as if I were looking through a pane of glass at nothing, or as if the world outside the window were a painting without people. I seem to myself like a little ghost, and I see my father's strained face, as I sometimes saw it in those days. What am I seeing? A premonition of depression, of agoraphobia? The aloneness which my father painted into his landscapes? But for him the paintings arose from happy concentration, from participation, being in nature, as he said. 'You have to love what you see: that's what being an artist means.'

Or I have followed in the footsteps of Richard Jefferies, 'moonin' about' and poking in hedges and ditches, as one of his contemporaries described him, with an active man's contempt for the contemplative? Something is sucking at the life inside me – a blackness is welling up. But what I want to see is the life out there, not my face reflected in the glass, or an empty landscape, but the quickness and the plenitude, in this common place.

27 November

At the end of *Passage to Juneau*, Jonathan Raban, having suffered the shipwreck of his broken marriage, quotes William Cowper's 'The Cast-Away': 'We perish'd, each alone'.

Reading this, the word 'alone', which sounds like a bell-buoy in the troubled waters of the poem, reminded me of John Cowper Powys's philosophy of aloneness. Powys makes it into a deeply positive thing, a sinking down of the individual soul upon nature, which is consonant with Wordsworth's 'The pleasure which there is in life itself'; and we may interpret Powys's last written word in this spirit.

There is another possibility, however. The Powyses were related to Cowper on their mother's side, and we know that John Cowper and Theodore, in particular, felt poor Cowper's fate keenly, and blamed it on God, taking the view that Cowper's God tormented him with the conviction of his damnation.

A feeling akin to madness is present in JCP's writings – in his neurotic confessions in *Autobiography*, and in the destructive, suicidal Powys heroes in his early novels, suicide remaining a preoccupation of his characters who resemble their author, though, with John Geard in *A Glastonbury Romance*, self-inflicted death becomes a means to life-enlargement rather than annihilation. Belinda Humfrey once speculated about the existence of an abyss of horror in Powys; and I have sensed something similar.

What I am wondering now is whether Powys, through a massive act of self-transformation, took the horror of aloneness, a horror equivalent to Cowper's conviction of damnation, and turned it into his sensationalist philosophy, his art of happiness, in which the solitary self achieves ecstasy through its communion with nature.

But my point is not that such a transformation conceals a greater truth, which we can expose by psychoanalysing Powys. On the contrary, what we learn from him is that psychoanalysis itself is a modern scientific superstition. There is no greater truth lurking in an 'unconscious' dimension; what we are is what we make ourselves, with our will and imagination.

As I understand it, this is the Powysian view. My feeling is that complete self-knowledge and complete knowledge of another person are equal impossibilities. With our mixed motives, with the knot of contradictions that we are, and with the relationships that make us, as beings subject to change, who live in time, there is no position from which we can gain complete self-knowledge. We are always on the inside of our own faces, and in life, so that ideas of the self tend to be waxwork ideas, perceptions of ourselves as effigies. It is in this context that, unlike Powys, I can accept the idea of God. I don't mean the love of God – I'm not here speaking religiously, and without love there is no religion. I'm speaking, rather, of an intellectual position, or perhaps I really mean a need that makes an idea possible: the need to think that, though we cannot fully know ourselves, there is a perspective in which we are fully known.

Richard, on the phone from college, told me of his shock at hearing that a body had been recovered from the lake at Newton Park, and his immediate thought that it was a student who had committed suicide. Then he learnt that the human remains were Roman, which isn't so surprising when one considers the many layers of human occupation on the Newton Park site.

The image of the Roman remains being drawn from the water invoked an image which haunted me when I was a child. Then, I was told that a Roman centurion had been found in Itchen mud at Clausentum, the Roman port within the area that became Southampton. And at once, and for ever after, I saw a pristine figure, a centurion fully armed, excavated from the mud, only more like wax than flesh, like an illustration in my book, *The Story of Britain in Pictures*.

The figure lives in my mind with an image my father gave me. When on his travels as a young man, he visited Malmesbury Abbey, and talked with some workmen who had, shortly before, opened a medieval stone coffin. They were shaken by what they had seen: a beautiful young woman who, even as they looked down on her, dissolved into dust.

Even in the late '40s and early '50s Pennington remained in touch with an older world. There were the old people, for example – farmer Smith and farmer Pardy, Archie Fugget, who lived alone with his sister who was deaf and dumb, and kept one cow, which roamed the village, so that he was always out seeking 'she'; there was Mrs Rendle, who lived across the road from us, and took in washing (I would look down from my bedroom window and see her crossing the road, her hair as white as the sheets she was carrying); there were Mr Bullard and Mr Swimmings, who was often to be seen standing about the village with a bible or prayer book in his hand, preaching to whoever would listen, which was usually only me. There were the Commons, too, Pennington Common and Wainsford Common, the former a large area of gorse and rough grassland close to the centre of the village, and the latter, rougher, wilder, separated from Pennington Common by a few fields and houses, and sloping down to Avon Water. Each was distinct – one formed a playground and served the function of a village green – the other was little used except by a few children, lovers, ponies and cows (including Archie's). Despite their differences, both commons were recognisably parts of the one landscape. Moreover, although outside the bounds of the New Forest, they were, topographically, parts of the Forest. I knew little about the bounds in those days, but I had read Arthur Conan Doyle's *The White Company*, and its medieval Forest, which included the coastal area from Southampton Water to Christchurch, was my New Forest.

Standing in Northover Road, we could see the blue flame at Fawley Oil Refinery. My father had augured the land on which the Refinery had been built. Tony and David had both had temporary jobs on its construction. The first American I met was a boy called Tex, whose parents bought the house next to Hayford, Penn Cottage, whose gate opened on Ramley Road; although they didn't live there long. Tex's father was an executive in the oil industry working at Fawley, and to my eyes Tex was amazing. He was just like a little man, with a suit and hat which made him a miniature version of his father. We set up a telephone line consisting of cotton reels, match boxes and thread, which trailed over the hedge and gardens, and connected our bedrooms, but didn't manage to communicate any messages.

Hayford was in the New Forest as far as I was concerned. The roads were unfenced then, and Forest ponies and cattle wandered into Northover Road and, if our gate was open, into the garden. One night we heard them out there, snorting and clomping the ground with their hooves, and Dad drove them out and closed the gate. Unfortunately, he missed some of them in the dark, and in the morning these were corralled in the garden, which was well churned up. Poorer or more frugal villagers used to collect dung from Pennington Common, shovelling it into wooden carts – boxes on pram wheels – and taking it home to use as manure in their gardens, and collecting gorse sticks to use on their fires.

'To be is to be in place,' according to the philosopher Edward S. Casey. I know it. It might be possible for me to describe the long straggling village, strictly speaking the two villages, Upper Pennington and Lower Pennington, extending from the marshes beside the Solent and opposite the Isle of Wight, towards Sway and the open Forest to the north, and eastward to Lymington, and towards Everton and Keyhaven in the west. No description, however, would be the place I knew, and although I can see its features clearly enough now, what matters to me is the place I was once part of, and which is part of me now; and that is the place which I can't see.

Across the fields at the end of Northover Road, past the house where Punch Browning lived, lay Yaldhurst – the old hurst, as I would later realize: once manorial land, with a large house and a few smaller ones, and a painted gipsy caravan, among woods and fields. But of course it was all new to us as boys. Luck was with me in my family and home ground, as it was later in my friends. And was then – children rarely seek any great intimacy with one another, it is enough to share the same games, the same adventures and explorations. But is this true? I remember my son as a little boy crying because Owen had told him he was no longer his best friend. I also had best friends, but when I think of friendship, it is of a later emotion, rooted in conscious sharing, rather than the pleasure I took in Charlie's company or Brian's or Roger's or David's, or even in the need I felt for Peter to like me.

The cold strikes my fingers with a thrill of newness as I hold the lamp of my bike, so that Roger and I can see the words of the carol we are singing, at the front door of a house at Yaldhurst. The night is black but sparkles with stars, an infinite number of tiny bright scintillations in the covering sky. I say we are singing, but in fact Roger is managing a less than tuneful noise, and I am groaning: 'O little town of Bethlehem'. On similar winter nights now the sensation comes back to me, with cold fingers, the feel of metal and plastic, and a small circle of lamplight. But the encompassing night is irrecoverable, and I stand outside looking in. Now too I think of holly in the depths of the Forest, dark red berries against spiny leaf crowns, which shine in winter sunlight, and the running of the deer. It returns to me as poetry rather than song, with the red of Rufus's hair and beard, and the red of his blood soaking the ground where he has fallen, at the foot of a giant, ribbed oak.

Again, I see myself running on the road through the woods near Boldre Church, gravel spurting from under my plimsoles. I am in the lead, with boys trailing behind me, and the Headmaster, a vigorous man in his thirties (but he smokes cigarettes), striving to overtake me, and saying 'Hooker never gives in'. Above us, the church appears on its hill surrounded by trees, the squat tower, and long low building, more like a tithe barn than a church. There is a painting of this building by my father – somewhere, it was hanging then in the dining room at Rope Hill. What haunts the church itself is another painting, and the event it commemorates: *HMS Hood*, and on a table below it, the Book of Remembrance, containing the names of all the sailors who died in the explosion. The fact itself haunts, and the contrast between the peaceful place, redolent of a picturesque idea of the Middle Ages, and the terrifying violence which, in a sense, it contains.

'The Road to Keyhaven' is another of my father's paintings. It is hanging on the wall of my study, where I am writing this. As the curved road tops a rise, alongside a white farmhouse, the blue whaleback of West Wight comes into view, and the whole atmosphere changes. I am cycling on the road, through Lymore, on the way to Keyhaven and Saltgrass Lane and Hurst shingle-spit, with a fishing rod tied to the crossbar and a bag jogging against my back. I am alone, or telling boastful fishing stories to my older fishing friends, Rod Saunders and Chugsie Orman, trying their patience. Or I am cycling back, through the woods beyond Everton, past the ruins of the mud-walled hovel disappearing into undergrowth, where the old woman used to live who drew her water from a spring beside the road, and had the reputation of being a witch. And now, through a gap between trees on my right, I see a wheatfield, and stop and dismount, astonished and afraid, because it isn't corn but a sea of liquid gold. And this is the same day when, arriving home, I hear Dad talking to Uncle Tom on the lawn among the apple trees, and he is saying: 'The Russians are strong, but the beauty of it is the Americans are stronger'.

But, quite possibly, memory has deceived me. It wasn't the same day that I saw the wheatfield, and my father wasn't talking to Uncle Tom but to another man, and I didn't feel a warm sense of security at my father's wisdom. I may have felt contempt, for this happened in the period when I had rejected my father's politics, and felt that he and all the old fools were leading us to annihilation. But that belongs to a time outside this story, and as I look, now, at 'The Road to Keyhaven' I am coming over the hill to the sight of the Island, and to a different air, and am too deeply in the painting to see myself or to be seen.

At times a memory is given back, or becomes a story which we think is true. Dad used to paint alongside his cousin Stewart, who was a well-known landscape painter. He also did a painting of Boldre Church, which is hanging on our wall downstairs. In old age, Stewart reminded me of the afternoon when he and Aubrey had set up their easels on the lawn at Hayford, and I was hiding behind a tree, and egged on by 'the old man' (my grandfather, Tom), was lobbing green apples at the canvases. 'Yes,' I said, 'I remember'; and how much I wanted to, sharing in Stewart's pleasure as he looked back through the years to that summer afternoon, which lived in his mind as it did not in mine. And yet, with the proffered picture, sensations began to form – the little old man grinning and whispering, the feel of the smooth-skinned green fruit, the action of lobbing…

Dad's studio, a wooden garden shed, stood on the lawn. As he was losing his sight, he would work at one of his paintings – one of the best, a study of Pennington Common – spoiling it, and I would sit at my desk in the room above, looking down at him, happy to see him absorbed in his painting, but wishing that it wasn't that particular painting he was ruining. Now, too, the wonderful garden at Hayford – his and Mother's work of art – was beginning to suffer. I would see him with a garden line in his hand, stretching it across the turned soil, but now it was no longer straight, but crooked, and he would be more likely to trample on vegetables than to pick them or dig them up – the softly bristling bunches of carrots, the gleaming, earth-caked spuds.

I once saw an artist who lived in a northern town being interviewed on TV. He said that his ambition was to live his whole life-cycle in the one place, painting what he saw. The words gave me an emotional shock, which I have never forgotten, because they spoke my own feelings exactly.

But of course, it isn't always possible to live the life one wants to, especially if one has to make a living, as my father and I after him had to do. Would he have lived a different life if he could, perhaps becoming a professional painter like his cousin Stewart? I don't think so: his work at the Ministry was important to him; he loved the land, and he had his gardening as well as his painting. When I knew that my parents would have to sell Hayford and move into a bungalow, I felt that I would like to burn the house down, as gipsies set fire to the caravan and its contents when one of their people, who owns it, has died. The strength of the feeling took me by surprise – it was so irrational, and there was nothing about it that I could approve of with my mind. As if in a selfish rage one would destroy what one could no longer have, or annihilate the place of memory, so that no one else, blind and indifferent to the memories, could make the place their own.

I didn't intend to visit the house ever again. But one day, having driven from our home in Somerset to the sea at Milford and Hurst shingle-spit, on the way back, I instinctively turned off Ramley Road into Northover Road. To this road, when it was a gravel track, I had run back from Pennington Common, because I had seen fire in the bedroom window, and not known that it was a reflection of the setting sun; or because I had remembered the old tale of the boy who wanders into an enchanted place, and, returning home after a short stay, finds that years have passed, and his whole family and everyone he knew has died long-since, and no one remains who has heard of him. Now, as I pulled up in the road outside the house, alongside the hedge which I had once set on fire, I saw that a new bungalow had been built across the lawn where my father's studio had stood, and the name on the gate had been changed. The house was now called Gardener's Cottage.

Afternoon. Completed the first rough draft of 'A Stroke of Luck'. Now I shall let it dry on the page while I finish revising 'Adamah' and get on with the critical book.

It will need a lot of revision, but the important thing is I got into the flow of it. Using the journal helped me to give the self-censor the slip. I was able to write what interested me, without thinking too much about self-presentation or worrying about the enormity – and possible disloyalty – of writing about my parents and brothers. Reflecting on fiction and the unreliability of memory actually enabled me to make autobiographical sketches. I think I've got some truth to sensation, which was the thing I was after.

Of course, it was myself too that I didn't want to betray. It's the life experience that can't be put into words. In consequence, the more vividly one writes the greater the risk of producing a painted waxwork. But to approximate, and in doing so to convey something of the life-sensation, when I thought about dying, it seemed important for me to attempt this.

29 November

A clouded still damp morning, the birch a filigree of silvery water drops which are more visible than the twigs; among them, a scattering of yellow leaves.

For the first time the other day, I noticed another yew tree, which I have been looking at for years. Visible through our front window, it stands, behind a stone wall, on the corner of Stevens Lane, opposite the site of the Asylum (which Jack remembered). From certain angles, it can be seen together with the other yew, in the paved area among the bungalows.

The two yews strengthen my suspicion that Sunnyside was once the site of an ecclesiastical building – a monastery or nunnery – with its burial ground. Mieke is as happy as I am in the house in which we live, but she is inclined to make a connection between the number of serious illnesses suffered by youngish people, including myself, in the houses, and some infection, possibly in the water, springing from contaminated ground. I can't quite say this is a superstition – and if it is, I too am not quite immune – though I argue that the number of illnesses is a coincidence, or perhaps even average for the population at large.

Certainly no one wants to think that they are living on infected ground! Frome is extraordinary for its character as an underground town. It has many cellars and is riddled with subterranean passageways, whose functions local historians dispute. Conduits which once carried water or sewage would seem to be the answer, though this may not explain all the hidden ramifications and connections. We too have a cellar – a cave with stone walls built like a castle – and although I don't think it conceals any passageways, I can't be sure.

The town below the town reminds me of other places – Acre, for example, or Winchester. In a way it's a microcosm of our English settlements – the palimpsest landscapes, the foundations upon foundations. It was the *poetry* of England that our American friend, the poet Barbara Moore, felt nostalgia for, though she had never visited England, and in any case it's only absent from America if one overlooks Native American cultures. But I knew what Barbara meant, and it was one of the things I missed most when living in upstate New York.

The old stone walls speak of it ... yet the idea of contamination is significant. My feeling for past-marked landscapes contains a periodic sense of suffocation, as though preceding generations have breathed all the air. It's less likely now to be caused by an oppressive determinism, since the new England of supermarkets & motorways & TV *seems* to have no connection to an older England. Albeit poets may think differently, as when Ted Hughes posits a Protestant/Catholic split in the English psyche, or David Jones laments our *lebensraum* in 'Brut's Albion'.

On my morning walk, turning into a narrow lane behind the bungalows, I saw that a young man whom I didn't know was walking towards me, and for an instant I hesitated, and almost turned back. It was a shadow of the old shyness, which, when I was a boy, used to make me cry when I was cycling down Ramley Road and another solitary cyclist – in those days of quiet roads – came towards me. It's very strange, this not wanting to be *seen*. Much as I've wanted a kind of success – to be known as a writer – I also shrink from any form of self-assertion.

This has some pride in it, like Dad not wanting to have an exhibition of his paintings, though I feel sure that if someone else had arranged one on his terms, and it had been well received, he would have been very pleased. But in me it has, too, some reaction against his emotional self-assertion, and the play-acting that was part of him. Mother said that, when they were first married, it was as though he was always on the stage.

There's a mystery about how one is in the world, how different people are. Because T. F. Powys lived the life of a hermit, Peter Riley said he was afraid of life. And perhaps Theodore was – it would depend what's meant by 'life'. Quite probably, TFP, with his highly original way of seeing things, equally in his life and art, shrank from conventional judgement, whether of Bloomsbury literati or Dorchester tradesmen. He would have been at home with friends who appreciated him, and villagers who only passed the time of day. And, after all, there is quite a lot in life that any thinking person is wise to be afraid of.

When I think of my father now, it isn't his playacting that I see, or any regret or resentment. I see him concentrated, completely absorbed, in the garden at Hayford, with a spade or line in his hand, or in his studio, in front of a painting, holding a brush or palette knife.

30 November

Bright sky appearing under cloud cover, over the Longleat woods. Touches of frost on grass and roofs.

Still almost December and no real cold yet. Stevie Davies, in a recent letter, responding to my 'Dragons in the snow': 'It's so grim that there isn't snow any more – none to speak of – to make us cold so that boys' hands can warm us. This endlessly mild weather makes me apprehensive, & the lack of seasons.' In his last years at Hayford Dad used to comment with disgust on the mild winters and their harmful effect on the soil.

Apart from the winter of 1947, the first cold I really remember was on early morning winter journeys to school at St Peter's, getting off the bus at Christchurch and waiting at the trolley terminus while the yellow flat-faced trolley was turned round and made ready to go back in the direction of Southbourne. Mornings of red ears burning with cold and gloved hands clasped together or held in pockets, but fingers tingling.

But memory pushes back memory. Earlier winters were real enough. At Rope Hill, for example, after a heavy fall of snow, riding behind Mr Arch on a toboggan, hurtling downhill towards the playing field, swerving to miss an oak tree and rolling over and over. The same year, with Quentin Ralston, careering down the hill at Buckland Rings, stopping just short of the barbed wire fence. Or earlier, staying at home from Rowan College because of a snowfall, throwing snowballs in the garden, and getting into trouble – unjustly – with other children who'd stayed away from school.

1 December

'You can be richer than God,' according to a City stockbroker. But who's poorer than a god who's not believed in?

This morning, at my desk, I watched a goldcrest flitting from twig to twig of the birch – sipping beads of moisture? A bluetit was active there too.

Roland John called in mid-morning for the second time in a week, bringing me books. Talking about poetry and the present dearth of good poetry criticism, we find a lot of common ground.

2 December

'I really believe that what we have announced today [the decoding of chromosome 22] will be used for the next thousand years. If you think of any other invention that has been used that long, you can really only think about the invention of the wheel.' (Dr Michael Dexter)

This morning, I drove the car for the first time since my stroke, only changing its parking place, but it felt good.

After several days of feeling ill and exhausted, Mieke has been drinking today. I too have been feeling ill with the same virus, though not as bad, and it hasn't stopped me working. Fearing she would make herself worse I spoke to her angrily, and she told me to 'fuck off' – which was fair enough.

As well as fear, the idea of self-inflicted sickness brings out in me a puritanical disgust.

3 December

Rain and strong wind singing in wires, blowing smoke from a chimney flat across a roof. I found walking difficult with the wind behind or in front of me – probably not much more so than I would do normally, but now I'm more anxious about the consequences of losing my balance.

Tree full of agitated starlings, whistling and clacking their beaks. A black cat, in high excitement, running along the path below.

4 December

The old lady who lives on the corner said to me this morning, 'You write poems don't you'. (She said 'pomes'.)

'Yes.'

'My niece has done a book about Somerset and the Titanic.'

'That sounds interesting.'

'I 'spect your pomes are too.'

I drove to the supermarket. Too fast, M. said. It was the sense of freedom.

The Leverhulme Trust has turned down my application for a grant to free me from academic duties so that I can work on 'poetry and the sacred'. The third time they've rejected my application. Not surprising, of course; my status wouldn't have carried any weight, even if the subject did.

But do I believe in my work?

Yes. But I'm not sure that I could justify it on 'academic grounds'.

I'm not certain that anything I've done could be justified on those grounds – even the teaching. As for the poetry, it was never a professional requirement that I write it. (If it had been, I might have done something else instead!)

Most of my work has been done *in spite of.*

Actually, a grant at this stage might inhibit me, I would feel obliged to concentrate on the critical project, whereas now I can write what I want to. And if the study of sacred poetry takes far longer, and even if I don't finish it, no matter – everything I write is round and about the subject anyway.

5 December

The pavement at the bottom of Culver Hill was sparkling with frost on a cold morning. As I was walking over it gingerly, Barry, a tall, thin figure in a t-shirt and shorts ran across the road and embraced me.

Mieke continues poorly, sleeping most of the time.

I am driving on with my chapter on John Cowper Powys. He makes something immensely complex out of his mythological landscapes, but it was really something quite simple that first appealed to me about him. Initially, a name and a photograph: 'old earth man', JCP sitting down on a ditch-bank, alone, and apparently deep in the country. I scarcely realised then, living as I was at Brynbeidog, how out of date in relation to the concerns of the twentieth century his books would seem to most people. But of course that isn't how I see them *now* either – only aspects of them. But I do think poetry of earth needs to draw on new resources, including the sciences which he opposed. Today, when scientific explanations of the nature of life seem to be widely accepted with superstitious awe, I often wonder what happened to the human imagination, which surely has something to do with how we apprehend life. But it is as if the human mind has no valid say in meaning, and can only receive the 'truth' that science reveals.

Now as I look out through the birch on a still afternoon, I can see only a very few leaves still clinging to twigs. So it really is winter at last, despite the mild weather here in the West Country.

7 December

Joe has now moved into an unfurnished maisonette at Woolston, with a view of the Itchen Bridge from the veranda.

Jonathan Raban rang me from Seattle last night, in response to the letter which I sent him via his publishers about his new book, *Passage to Juneau*. We talked for some time, mainly about fishing and writing. My first published poem. 'Tench Fisher's dawn', which appeared in *Encounter*, was dedicated to him, in celebration of our dawn visits to the lower lake at Walhampton. The dedication was removed at the suggestion of the editor when the poem was published, presumably because Jonathan's name wouldn't have meant anything to the reading public at that time.

On my walk this morning, on two sticks, an old man using one stick greeted me and asked about my disability. He has seen me walking about, and says I'm doing very well.

Gulls crying over the gardens. Is there anywhere in England, however far inland (but nowhere is very far), that they don't bring a sound of the sea?

14 December

Cold bright winter morning. Frozen beads of moisture on twigs & branches. Leaf spray frost patterns on car bonnets & windscreens. Pavement sparkling in the sun.

I had dreamed of a poetry reading. First a woman who didn't know them, and a man who was learning English, read my poems alternately, and very badly. Then I tried to read them and couldn't; the lines fragmented on the page. I spoke to the small audience – Raymond Stephens, Tessa Hadley, Belinda Humfrey, and a few others: 'Sometimes I'm tired of poetry. Tired of words'. With an attempt at a lighter tone: 'Tired of life.'

During the day I had been feeling tired, and weary at the thought of going back to college in January. Heavy thoughts: thirty years teaching with little reward; more hard work to come. And will I be up to it now?

The usual litany of complaint, brought on by the prospect of going back, and uncertainty about whether I'll be able to cope; and perhaps also because I had worked hard completing my chapter on J. C. Powys, and had prepared my new collection of poems to send to Stephen at Enitharmon.

So it hadn't been an unprofitable period of convalescence.

What reward does one expect? Surely I've understood by now that there's none to be looked for, except in the work itself. And maybe I've learnt something at last: to do the teaching required of me as well as I can, but to put my own writing first.

15 December

In my dream Dad was thinning the hedge in front of a house opposite Northover Road. He was going at it in his way, with furious determination, which made me anxious in case the owners of the house objected. I was also concerned that the wheelbarrow projected out into the road, so I moved it up the bank, where it listed precariously. This is just as he was when there was hard work to be done in the garden. He made me feel angrily redundant when he 'helped' me take out a hedge in the garden at Brynbeidog. Dave used to snort with indignation as he told me about Dad pressurising him to do 'a hard slog' in the garden.

Walking to the post office just now, to post the typescript of *Adamah* to Stephen, and feeling the burden of my slowness, I remembered a night when, drunk, I walked back past St Thomas's church in Lymington and saw the church clock as a yellow face, which became an image in a poem that I wrote.

Poetry begins in separateness, or is an expression of it, in our society. Not in any society, but in ours, or societies like ours, where individuality is valued. It may become a curse, too, or be the rankest conventionality, with thousands of people each expressing the same individual separateness.

While Dave reacted strongly against 'culture' as his father embodied and cherished it, Tony and I both found pleasure and meaning in it, Tony more so, in a way: in his love of opera and Brechtian theatre, for example. He made me feel something of a barbarian with my anti-social bookish habits, and fear of public spaces, such as theatres.

How hard is it now for anyone who values culture in this sense, as distinct from popular culture, which is the kind most noticed and most honoured even by institutions (the BBC, 'quality' newspapers, universities) one would have once expected to hold the values my parents held. How isolated they would have felt. I doubt they would have understood the fear of appearing 'elitist' that haunts highly educated people today.

Having imbibed their idea of culture, and working in the present climate, I often wonder what I'm doing writing the kinds of poems I write. There's no choice: I write out of necessity, but I often wonder about the idea of culture – of Europe, of civilization – that's implicit in most of what I write. Once it seemed enough to get excited by an image – to see things at an imaginative angle, finding my separateness in a view of the world. But for a long time now there's been a question over why I write.

Of course the pressure of my whole experience in Wales, in which there is still a strong sense of the poet as a voice of the community, bears on me in this respect. But I can't go back to that; and living in Wales never meant claiming to be part of something I wasn't part of. I think there are things I can't work out, questions I can't answer, because I am *in* the situation, not an observer of it from the outside. Yet if I didn't ask the question I wouldn't be alive to the situation.

What use *is* poetry that isn't popular now?

17 December

Had a meal with Colin Edwards at The Horse and Groom, East Woodlands, the other night. There, beyond the town lights, we stepped out of the car under a beautifully clear night-sky. How I wish I could identify more of the stars! How ironical that one knows so little of this vast universe – though naming alone isn't knowing.

Colin told me his daughter Isobel had been a shepherd in her school nativity play. The local paper this week is full of photographs of children in nativity plays in their primary or infant schools. I remember Joe & the other children at Llangwyryfon. This seems to me now the best of Christmas, the truest spirit, among all the consumerist noise & glitter – louder & brighter this year because of the imminence of the millennium.

The nativity chimes with our feeling for an older world: shepherds keeping watch in the fields, wise men following the star, birth of a child in a stable, warm-scented with hay & the breath of beasts.

Therein lies the problem: that one's love & awe are invested in nostalgia for something that's no longer part of our world. I know it in my own case, looking back to the farming that still existed in my childhood after the war. And in today's THES there's an article called 'A day in a farmer's life, 2015', which imagines the farmer spending his day in front of a computer, while satellites & sub-soil sensors report on the work that needs to be done, most of it by robots.

It has seemed to me in recent years that life may be coming to an end on this planet. And, of course, it may – human life, because of our inability to live at peace with one another or in harmony with nature. But I am aware, too, that life as I have known it is undergoing immense change – always granted that I was born into an older world, through my parents' memories & values, and Mother's feeling for family history.

In one sense, this feeling is no new thing. At 18, I was acutely conscious that the world might end through nuclear war. But in another sense, it is; because of the network of new communications systems that seem to penetrate every aspect of existence. Everywhere the margin of mystery retreats further, yet fundamental ignorance of ourselves & nature remains. We know everything and nothing.

What is new is the end of nature. I understand full well what Bill McKibben means, in spite of my contrary argument about ditch-vision. Nature doesn't end, as I know simply by looking out of the window, where tiny finger-like catkins stand out on the birch twigs, which are beaded with rain drops. What does end is the older story of nature: in America, the tale of wilderness; in Europe, the pattern of agriculture which, until recently, remembered the shepherds & the birth in the stable.

But this too is a local perspective based on an affluent lifestyle. There are plenty of parts of Europe, and of America, without affluence, and some, in the former Soviet Union, where war & terror are as murderous as when Herod had the children slain or the Romans gave Jesus to be crucified.

Things do change, and the temptation to escape into nostalgia is great; but it is always the same darkness, however bright the world with its new illusions of light.

18 December

We were to have gone to Southampton to visit Joe in his new accommodation today but Mieke is ill; she still hasn't recovered from the virus.

Looking out of the window just now, I was surprised to see that it's snowing. Wet flakes falling crisscross, now driving slant across the gardens, fields beyond the roofs whited out. Suddenly, with this fall, winter seems more real here.

The main news yesterday was that many more people may be incubating the CJD virus. Scientists don't know how many, or when – in 3 or 30 years – those carrying the disease will begin to show symptoms, and to die. They speak of it as a 'time bomb' inside us – and since no one knows who the 'us' are, everyone can feel apprehensive.

This is highly ironic in relation to what I was thinking about yesterday, of course. On the one hand, predictions of a robotized agriculture which, with hardly any physical labour, will provide for the needs of an enlarged and mainly urban, affluent population. On the other, fears & uncertainties comparable to those of an age of plague.

The snow seems to have thickened in the short time since I started writing. There are streaks among the small flakes – but even as I watch, it seems to slow, and become thinner again. It's hopeless trying to record such a thing.

There's something about watching or thinking about snow falling, from within a sheltered, comfortable position, that induces a sense of great peace. James Joyce knew this, as he shows at the end of 'The Dead'. What is it? Is it an idea of death, like rain falling on the just and the unjust alike? A kind of blanket of unconsciousness, which in imagination we can draw over all our troubles, and cover the whole of humanity, the living and the dead, as grassy mounds enfold the ancient dead on the downs.

It brings a dream state to the day. Hypnotic as the approach of sleep, or like the atmosphere of a dream, without cause or effect, in a way mirroring our life experience, as awareness dawns after the darkness of birth, and as darkness will fall again.

This snow won't settle, I think. It's too wet for that. Already it's falling differently – straighter, thinner. But there's a white edge to the slate roof I can see through a side window, and white on the solitary, green moss-mole.

19 December

I was wrong, the snow has settled, not deep, but more than usual for this part of the country now, before Christmas.

We walked out carefully on a clouded morning, the frosted snow bluish-white and sparkling. A transfiguring brightness about everything, houses, trees, Cley Hill (more misty white) across the fields. Children were shouting with pleasure as they tobogganed down the slope in front of Sunnyside Place, where, before today, it wouldn't have occurred to me that it would be possible to slide.

It's fascinating, sometimes, to learn how other people (including friends) see one. Thus Kim Taplin, in the new edition of *The English Path*, says my 'poetry continues in its devotion to the task of ruminative praise'.

Which makes me feel like a cow chewing the cud; and reminds me of Welsh friends inclined to assign to me a secure sense of 'English' identity. But it's partly true, as I can see when I think of the poems Kim has in mind – in the main poems of friendship, from Moor Farm, or walking with Jim at Pitts Deep. The other part of the truth is the one that readers often miss – the radical insecurity, and the attachments held against pressures (social & cultural as well as personal) working against them.

One thing is certain: however the future may describe one, if it has any occasion to, it won't be in terms in which one would describe oneself. But that isn't to say I'm not grateful to Kim, who has been one of my closest readers over the years.

* * *

'Śiva is a destroyer and loves the burning ground. But what does He destroy? Not merely the heavens and earth at the close of a world-cycle, but the fetters that bind each separate soul. Where and what is the burning ground? It is not the place where our earthly bodies are cremated, but the hearts of His lovers, laid waste and desolate. The place where the ego is destroyed signifies the state where illusion and deeds are burnt away: that is the crematorium, the burning ground where Śri Natarāja dances, and where He is named Sudalaiyādi, Dancer of the burning-ground.'
     Ananda K. Coomaraswamy, *The Dance of Siva*

'Destroy, because all creation proceeds from destruction … For all building up is done with debris, and nothing in the world is new but shapes. But the shapes must be perpetually destroyed … Break every cup from which you drink.'
     Marcel Schwob,
     quoted in Coomaraswamy

Late afternoon on a freezing day. A shaft of golden light on the stairs, as the sun goes down behind workshop roofs on the Marston Trading Estate and behind the line of the Mendips, bringing out the dark, fine-boned look of distant trees. Big waxing moon over the downs.

I seem to be moving more freely now, although that may be due to the care I had to take this morning, leaving round marks from the rubber ends of sticks beside my footprints in the snow. But I do come and go more easily on the stairs, and scarcely even think about using sticks in the house now; quite different from when I crept up to the spare room to look at Dad's pictures and the view of the hills.

My task now is to write about Alun Lewis, to try to say what I mean by his 'poetic courage' & the struggle within himself which he eventually lost in India – if the idea of 'loss' applies in a situation of general chaos.

20 December

Towards dusk: outside, a frozen landscape under a dull sky, which looks like more snow, the only bright thing my red jersey hanging upside-down on the line, arms reaching down to the ground.

Inside, I've worked at my desk, thinking about Alun Lewis and his 'darkness', which is a whole inner and outer landscape, in effect a poetic language in which he situates himself, and with which he seeks to express his depression & his sense of mystery. Again, I have the feeling of a poet whose fate is enfolded in his language – for whom there's no way out. As perhaps there wasn't anyway for a soldier-poet who knew the risk he was taking. But that isn't quite what I mean: there's death that eventually enfolds all, soldiers or not, and there's how we understand ourselves and the whole 'theme' of life and death. In Lewis's case, I have a feeling of terrible sadness, and waste, which he himself was guiltily aware of; but also of something like exhilaration, in the rhythmic & sonorous language in which he renounced the world.

'Being a romantic,' he said, with self-mocking irony. But as with Edward Thomas there's also the question of whether organic & elemental language, detached from its religious base, is capable of generating communal meanings, or whether the song of ultimate aloneness – the death song – is intrinsic to it.

21 December

I see in the paper this morning that Gwyn Jones has died. He was a very old man who had lived a vigorous life.

I never met him but I had a strong sense of his presence when I first went to Aberystwyth. He had left the department to go to Cardiff the year before, and my colleagues were divided in their feelings towards him. I received the impression of a giant of a man, vital & colourful & outspoken, to whom some had responded with love and others with fear, if not hate. In the main, I was drawn to those who loved him.

Christmas Eve

Mieke continuing very poorly – she's had a rotten month – I went to the supermarket alone this morning and did our Christmas shopping. Afterwards I took the car again and made two further excursions into Frome, threading my way through the crowds, and, on the second occasion, buying one of the last Christmas trees still available. By this time it was raining, as it is now, the trees outside my window thrashing in a wet & windy dusk.

Christmas Day

Snow fell in the morning, big wet flakes. It didn't settle here, but the high ground of Longleat and the Mendips was greyish white.

Joe rang early; he had been up since five playing Father Christmas. He sounded as happy as he said he was, with Maddy & Chlöe in his own new home. I should say theirs, but Maddy still has her caravan, and hasn't tired of the travelling life.

Boxing Day

Emily & Jason came over in the morning. Joe arrived with Maddy and Chlöe after them. Then Bethan & Ard, unexpectedly – they'd phoned from Brighton – bringing two friends, a young couple from Groningen. So the kitchen table was drawn out to its fullest length and we enjoyed a happy family meal together.

John Barnie, in the latest issue of *Planet*, writes that it is 'certain ... that the past, meaning the accumulated history and cultural inheritance of medieval and humanist Europe, is dead, not so much because it is handed down to us in a dead language like Classical Greek or Latin, as because it is framed within a matrix of ideas, perceptions and beliefs about humans and the world that are no longer believable and therefore no longer open to use in our times'. What depresses me about this is the certainty of a kind of Dawkins-speak, the superstition of materialistic scientism to which all other thought-worlds are superstitions. That, and the feeling that Barnie may be right.

At the same time I've been reading a biography of Christina Rossetti with growing anger at the Christianity with which she seems to have maimed herself. If that is the religion we have lost, good riddance. Of course, I know it isn't only that; but sometimes the sick & violent life-denial fills my whole field of vision.

Barnie is worrying over the future of art – what it will draw on in order to reach people in the next millennium. He is a bold generaliser; he thinks that 'death of feeling' – 'numbness' – is 'this century's true legacy to the future'. Maybe that is so. I know what he means; but I also suspect that he has numbed himself with an excess of neo-Darwinist dogmatism.

A lot of feeling, I would say, has gone into women's work. Which is where it has always been, but now (as a result of the women's movement) with a broader based, more confident articulateness. The answer to male aggression is explicit now, whereas in 19th century English writing it tended to be more implicit and indirect. Neo-Darwinist certitude is one of the pillars of male dogmatism in our time, and it has a lot to answer for as far as the numbing of feeling is concerned. For if human creativity counts for so little there isn't much use for feeling.

It isn't the whole edifice of Christian culture whose loss I fear. For with that would go the terrible cruelties & maiming denials that are part of it. The loss I fear is that of the human soul, or, if the word is over-freighted with dogma, the personal culture in men and women: the imagination: the exploratory mind: that which makes a person seek meaning in experience, or partly seek it and partly make it.

1 January

Well, here it is, the year 2000.

We spent the last evening of the old year/millennium with Colin & Ros & Isobel, and Richard & Tracey at Freshford, but came home at 10.30, when they went to a party at the village hall. So we saw in the New Year together, with fireworks exploding and colouring the sky all round.

This morning it was mild and misty here with a ghost sun. We walked through Keyford to Gore Hedge. This was where the bodies, or parts of the bodies, of local men executed after the Battle of Sedgemoor were displayed, and I used to think the name referred to their blood. But apparently *gore* is an Anglo-Saxon word meaning hedge so that it refers to a boundary, and the name is a tautology (like Avon Water). New houses stand on the site now, opposite Wesley Slope and the large, square Wesley Methodist church. From here we walked on Christchurch Road East, which runs parallel to the town centre in the valley below, St John's spire rising out of mist. Then up Alexandra Road to Locks Hill and so home.

I don't feel that I'm walking any better than I was a month or six weeks ago. My legs feel stiff and heavy. But this was our longest walk so far: it's probably a mental attitude I have to overcome now, because I'm not making as much progress as I thought I would – and of course I have to push myself and go on exercising.

How different this Millennium – the world lit up and visible in every part through electronic images – from what the last one must have been like. And which of these will the next one more resemble, I wonder.

Time is so unreal outside the human sphere. Beyond a certain point it is impossible to imagine. Scientists speak impressively of the billions of years of the earth's existence, but what we can really imagine is the human experience we can feel with, from the age of the cave paintings. So the impressive talk means very little. They may say the time of human life on earth is a tiny fraction of the time of life itself, but what we really know are the centuries, and the lifetimes. One lifetime of human experience has a fullness that determines qualitative time, compared to the desert vastnesses of countless millennia.

So however different or however much the same human life in 3000 will be, we will probably seem as distant to the people then as our apocalyptic ancestors seem to us.

But if anything bridges the distance it will be some essentially human voice or image.

According to an editorial in yesterday's *Guardian* the historian J. M. Roberts says in an account of the twentieth century: 'The core of western civilisation, articulated or not, would come to lie in belief in the promise of manipulating nature. In principle, that civilisation now asserts that there is no problem that need be regarded as insoluble, given sufficient resources of intellect and money; it has room for the obscure, but not the essentially mysterious'.

So there is the final boundary of human thought: between those for whom a problem may be obscure, but is soluble by scientific means, and those who believe that life is essentially mysterious.

And perhaps the last carrier – the last refuge of God – is death. If it could be *proved* that there's no afterlife – no spirit world – that there is nothing that's not material, there would be no mystery.

Is that true? Wouldn't the difference between man and woman remain, if in no way obscure, magical? And nature, and our life in nature?

As long as there are human beings with whom we, at this turn of a millennium, could identify, life will be magical. But could it be so without essential mystery, if we knew for certain that outside material existence there is nothing?

Death itself can come to seem a great refuge. With the world completely illuminated technologically, a single communications system, with nowhere remaining that could produce one of the old ghost stories, no darkness to generate a sense of awe; only death to make us wonder … But this is quite contrary to my way of thinking. This is the way of morbid retreat.

Life is centred in mystery. For all the light that floods the world now, we all live in darkness, poets & scientists alike. Only if we stop thinking and feeling will mystery cease. Only when *our* knowledge fills the whole universe, leaving no possibility of not knowing, or thinking outside it. And what human discovery could make that day come?

As for *manipulating* nature, the idea is barbarous. However much we still have to learn from nature, and to derive (in medicine, for example) from use of natural resources, the idea of a manipulative relationship to nature should be as untenable as Baconian torture.

2 January

A mild, even warm morning. Sparrows active round house eaves, chirping. A thrush singing.

After yesterday's complaint I found I could walk more easily this morning – to begin with, anyway – and walked without sticks as far as the bottom of Culver Hill, but with M. alongside me, carrying the sticks, which I knew I could use at any time. All the same, an advance.

The new millennium has begun in the West with the consumerist religion flourishing. It is passivity that's killing the human mind, the vast entertainments industry that would turn us all into passive receivers. But at no time is there more loneliness.

We talked about this this morning, sickened by the common assumption that everyone must be suffering from a hangover after the festivities. M. says passivity causes sickness; atrophy of the creative mind leads to psychosis, drug-taking, artificially stimulated excitement; in which case a whole way of life is self-condemned.

It's as if the old trope of the mind as a mirror has been revived, but with a difference. We are expected to be glassy reflectors, all dreaming the same popular dream of more money to buy more things. No one is to make any mental effort; even the New Labour idea of education seems to be old Gradgrind – fill and test young minds to fit them for the technological world they will inhabit. Creativity becomes the means to adaptation.

I should rejoice at the people of the world – or many of them – singing and waving to each other, welcoming in the new age of hope. And I do – but if only all the lights were turned off for five minutes, and everyone observed the same silence, and we each of us thought or prayed.

Then talked to each other, refusing the words put into our mouths by entertainers & advertisers & politicians; talked of our findings, shared our questions, looked deep into our hearts and minds to speak of the things that are real to us. And out of all shape hope that ignores the cacophonous, glitzy dream.

6 January

Dusk on another benign January day.

I've just completed the fourth chapter of 'Imagining Wales', on ideas of Welsh & English in the poetry of R. S. Thomas, David Jones and Gillian Clarke. This puts me a little ahead of where I hoped to be at this time, but quite a lot remains to be done.

7 January

This morning I drove into college with M., as a kind of test before returning to work next week. Only a few people about – all pleased to see me – the campus quiet, a pastoral haven on a mild, springlike day. It all seemed so pleasant & peaceful, I felt quite nostalgic for the old way of life, but apprehensive too, and, afterwards, tired.

8 January

To Woolston, to see Joe & Maddy in their maisonette on the Pear Tree estate, blocks of apartments round a green, built in the 1950s. Joe has painted the living room and they have made Chlöe's room bright & attractive, and are at work on the other rooms. It was lovely to see them in their own home, more spacious than a caravan, and more settled.

Before driving across town to see Jim we went the short distance to where the old floating-bridge used to be, the slipway now under the beautiful curve of the new Itchen Bridge. A kind of monument marks the place: a large brick-built bell-shape with a ratchet wheel and length of chain attached to the top; in front of it, nearer the water, an arch like a lych gate. Gulls on the water, suddenly a large flock, as kids started throwing them bread. A container ship going seawards. Across the river we could see the spire of St Mary's and, behind it, the Civic Centre tower. Puffs of white cloud in a blue sky. I remembered, when I was six years old, coming here by bus or car from Warsash in the morning, crossing over on the old floating-bridge, fascinated by the chains disappearing into the water.

Late afternoon. M. & I drove to Milford and, without forethought, booked into Westover Hall Hotel, a grand Victorian mansion, with oak panelling & stained glass, overlooking Christchurch Bay & the Isle of Wight. After dark we went down onto the sea front and looked at the stars over the sea. Lights on the Island, lights far to the west, on Purbeck, and, nearer, Bournemouth. An aeroplane's lights winking among the stars. Red-green, red-green, off the Needles. On the beach below us, a small, soft pool of lamplight where two fishermen were fishing. And still it was a large darkness, larger for the sea and the *hush* of the long waves – white in spite of the dark – along the shore.

9 January

Morning view from the veranda over the sea garden, light frost on grass. Sun rising over the Island, enveloped in an aura of sunlit sea mist, the long rounded back from west of Yarmouth to Alum Bay and the Needles, Tennyson's memorial on the highest point.

After breakfast we walked through the garden – brick path onto rough grass, area with pristine pines, dark green against a cloudless, pale blue sky, and gorse bushes – to low cliffs and onto a shingle beach. Distant chalk cliffs of Purbeck – end of the broken geological bridge – echoing the nearer cliffs of West Wight.

Sea music! Waves coming in, rising, concave waves curving over, breaking on shingle, ploughing it up – a long noise as water retreating sucks back the shingle, sifting, sifting…

Nothing looks purer than the foam. But that's an illusion, of course. Think of oil spreading on the Brittany coast now, after the breakup of a tanker; and the tar that has been part of this coast for as long as I can remember.

But the pure look itself is beautiful.

Shells among the pebbles, crab carapaces, straps of wrack, dog whelk egg-sacs.

Even now, a creation morning feel about the sea! Hurst shingle spit drenched in sea water & light.

10 January

A collared dove on top of a frosty fence near the bird table. Sidles back and forth, stretches its neck, balances, eyeing the table, wanting to eat, but watchful & anxious, afraid to go in under the little wooden roof. What it must be like, on a cold morning, to be so near yet so far, knowing instinctively the perils of accepting human hospitality!

The weekend away wasn't about the past, but about family and friends in the present, but it reminded me, as such visits usually do, of how much is compacted into the area where I was brought up and used to live. In the journey from Southampton into the New Forest and to the coast. In the city itself – kids playing by the water, commercial shipping, pleasure craft, the streets, the areas which are now almost wholly Asian – and Joe speaks angrily of whites who refuse to be housed in them. The sumptuous hotel we stayed in – late Victorian money & taste – a comic story of 1930s English snobbery: William Morris (Lord Nuffield) sold the home after only two years as its owner, Milford Golf Club having turned down his application for membership on account of him being in 'trade'. This England!

When we visited Jude & Peggy, Jude talked about sarsen stones in the old graveyard of Hordle church, close to Hordle House, which was a Prep School against which I played football for Rope Hill – memories of muddy knees & humiliating defeat (boys behind the goal taunting me: 'goalie not so popular now', after, having made several saves, I let in the eighth goal).

I saw so much from the top of the bus between Pennington and Christchurch, which I used to take on the journey to and from St Peter's. Always the sea view over Milford & Hordle cliffs thrilled me, and I would imagine myself on the beach fishing beyond the surf. I identify this route with seeing itself, from the time that I began to read Jefferies. The autumn & winter tints of the woods, the spring & summer colours, beside the road between Hordle and the turning to Barton, were to me a piercing feeling. A little later, the journey was enchanted by my passion for a young woman called Elsa Allen, who used sometimes to travel on the bus between Christchurch and Highcliffe, joking with my delightful, witty, foul-mouthed school friend Nicky Gossip and putting me to confused silence.

Now, I think I could live the rest of my life with M. walking in all weathers on the cliffs or beach at Milford or Hordle or the shingle-spit. But of course, a poet's work is to do with language, living speech, not just looking and forming visual images. Looking for 'treasure in rubbish heaps', being 'an archaeologist of the spirit', my art 'a museum', as Tony Conran, in a piece in *New Welsh Review*, would have it? It was the life here I longed to return to, and in a sense never left (though I had to grow up, and away), not the naked landscapes. And how could they ever be naked, for all the elemental beauty of rock and sea and light?

Even as a boy, I was in spirit an archaeologist, reading Christopher and Jacquetta Hawkes's *Prehistoric Britain*, the slim blue paper-covered Pelican, almost as dear to me as *Jefferies' England*, as I travelled on the bus to school. (And then a book by Leonard Woolley that made me realise archaeology was a science and therefore not for me). In a way, growing up was like growing into the past, or learning that the present rests on deep strata of past time. One way or another, this was a datum of experience I had to deal with, as other artists and writers have had to do, and others will, because the past is *there*, in the landscape & buildings, in the stories we tell or are told, in ourselves. *There*, and at the same time changing, as knowledge and angle of vision change; as person and world change through the relations they form with one another. If the past stands like the gravel and clay cliffs, like the cliffs it is always being eroded, exposing hidden deposits, falling, forming new configurations. Every morning the light of creation morning; earth and sea ancient, worked over, unstable – the instability itself a ground of new beginnings.

11 January

First working day back in college. Drive in fairly smooth – hold-ups make me anxious about needing to relieve myself – except for the usual go-slow at Rush Hill. (How Les used to fume; he was a man who had to be on the move.) MA poetry workshop from 10-1 with a coffee break at 11. A group of five, one man & four women, all interested, ready to talk. I was apprehensive to begin with, but found myself carried along as the class proceeded. Outside the workshop I met several colleagues whom I hadn't seen since the summer, and they welcomed me back warmly.

The small, cramped office which I share with Greg Garrard, who wasn't in today, smells of cat piss. Leaving the door open briefly, I discovered why, when I returned and found William, the big white cat that's often in or around the building, under my desk. All the same, and despite the college's lack of facilities, I was glad to be back.